BUDAPEST

2. The Illuminated Chronicle — a codex of history from the 14th century (National Széchényi Library)

THE HISTORY OF BUDAPEST

The soul of a city lies in its history. *Budapest* was several times ruined during the centuries, and had to be rebuilt again. What remained after the devastation was expropriated by the conquerors and converted to serve their own purposes. The Roman amphitheatre at *Aquincum* became the headquarters of the chieftain of the conquering Magyars, the stones of the fortress at Contra Aquincum, on the other side of the Danube, were used to build the houses of *Pest*. Medieval churches in Buda were converted into mosques by the Turks, bathhouses into Turkish baths. After the recapture of the city, the churches were recreated in a triumphant Baroque style. At the end of the

last century some architects used Romanesque and Gothic elements, others aimed at creating a national style. Naturally, none of these endeavours could be entirely successful, but all of them added something to the unique appearence of the city — Budapest.

In one of the caves on Castle Hill, prehistoric man had settled some half a million years ago and the capital city has been inhabited ever since for longer or shorter intervals. It is the traces of Illyrian (500—400 B.C.) and Celtic (300—60 B.C.) cultures in the first place that have been excavated by archaeologists. The first Golden Era of the region is associated with the appearance of the Eravisci, a tribe of Celtic origin. Their rule ended with the conquest of the Romans in 11 B.C. For the next four centuries it was the line of their fortresses — the *limes* — that marked the border of the Roman Empire. *Aquincum*, the site of the

◁ 1. The coat of arms of Budapest — 1873

Roman camp was occupied at the beginning of the 5th century by the Huns. These were followed by the Eastern Goths, Gepids, Lombards and, between 570 and 800 A.D., the Avars. The conquering Magyars settled in this territory in the late 9th century. Around *Contra Aquincum*, the Roman fortress at the ferry on the Pest side, a merchants' settlement was created, the nucleus of what was to become the city of Pest.

Until 955 A.D. the seat of the ruler was *Óbuda,* and subsequently the cities of Esztergom and Székesfehérvár. Despite this, however, *Buda* preserved its importance as a centre of power. The castle began to develop in the 12th century, this process being later interrupted by the Mongol invasion. The Mongols had invaded Pest in 1241 and during January of the following year they crossed the frozen River Danube and ruined Buda. After the capitulation of the Mongol army, King Béla IV settled the inhabitants of Buda and later the burghers of Pest, on Castle Hill. The settlement was surrounded by walls. Its increasing significance is marked by the fact that from 1346 onwards, King Louis the Great of the Anjou dynasty held his seat in Buda, and built the first royal castle there.

The Golden Age came with the reign of Sigismund of Luxembourg, the Holy Roman Emperor. He built a Gothic palace, fortified the defence system of the castle and had the whole of the royal castle surrounded by walls. During the reign of King Matthias Corvinus, the court of the great Renaissance ruler became a centre of culture and art famous throughout the whole of Europe.

The 150 years of Turkish rule after the battle of Mohács in 1526 put an end to this period of prosperity. The city was burnt up, the castle plundered and the former luxurious royal seat turned into a garrison on the border of the Ottoman Empire. After the recapture of Buda in 1686, new life

3. Pest and Buda in 1617 (National Széchényi Library)

4. *Buda Castle and the Chain Bridge in the 19th century (Kiscell Museum)*

slowly rose from the ruins and the city once again started to grow. Settlers, mostly German and Serb, erected modest Baroque burghers' houses. The first construction wave in high Baroque style did not occur until the reign of Queen Maria Theresa.

Pest gradually developed too, from 1767 on Theresatown — named after the Queen — was built, and the construction of Josephtown — named after her son — began in 1780. It was then that the leading role of Pest as opposed to Buda became obvious.

In 1873, the three cities, Buda, Óbuda and Pest were united under the name Budapest, which turned into one of the most rapidly developing metropolises in Europe. Embankments, railway stations, theatres, schools and housing estates were built at a fast pace. Brightly-lit cafés

mushroomed up all over the city, the telephone network began to spread and the first automobile appeared in 1895.

The millenium of the Magyar Conquest saw the construction of many opulent buildings. Vajdahunyad Castle, the Art Gallery, the Museum of Applied Art, Francis Joseph Bridge were inaugurated at this period. Development continued at the same speed after the millennial celebrations. An elegant district with office buildings came into being in the Inner City, with buildings like the Stock Exchange (now the headquarters of the Hungarian Television), the National Bank, and the building of the former Postal Savings Bank. Neo-Classic houses flanked the Danube, and the Houses of Parliament were constructed.

Development was first stopped by the First World War

and further hindered by the economic crisis that followed the collapse of the Austro-Hungarian Monarchy. After the Peace Treaty at Trianon a good fifteen years were to elapse before the economy slowly began to show signs of any improvement whatsoever. During World War II Hitlerite leadership and their Arrowcross-men in Hungary turned the country into a battlefield. All the Danube bridges were blown up and during the last-ditch fights the bulk of the buildings also perished.

In the spring of 1945, reconstruction started without delay and with great enthusiasm. It is thus a city rebuilt and reborn after disaster that waits for and welcomes visitors from all over the world.

BUDA CASTLE

As an old Italian saying has it: 'Europe has three gems — Venice on the water, Buda in the hills and Florence in the plain'.

The enthusiasm of the medieval chronicler is easy to understand. In the 14th-15th centuries Hungary was a great military, political and economic power, and a luxurious capital city.

In the 13th century, during the reign of King Béla IV the construction of Buda Castle began. The Palace, built by King Louis the Great and Sigismund of Luxembourg, witnessed its Golden Age under King Matthias Corvinus, the great ruler of the Renaissance. The 'Roman Hall' of King

5. A map from the beginning of the 19th century (Kiscell Museum)   *6. Panorama of Budapest* ▷

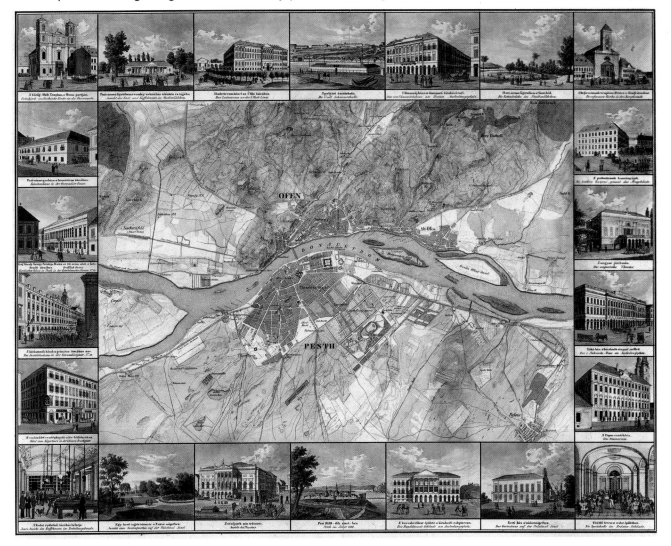

7. The façade of the Castle as seen from the Danube

Sigismund, with its 100 steps long and 25 steps wide interior, was a source of enchantment for visitors.

King Matthias extended and rebuilt the palace of his predecessors in an opulent style renowned all over Europe. He built a huge red marble staircase flanked by chandeliers. Gilt bronze statues were erected around the castle and the ornamental fountain in the courtyard was decorated with the statue of Pallas Athene as defender of the city. The chapel of the palace had an organ, a rarity at the time. It was here that the King kept the Byzantine reliquary of St John of the Alms, acquired from the Turkish Sultan. Italian, German and Hungarian masters worked at the reconstuction of the king's residence. The halls were decorated with finely carved white marble fireplaces, red marble doorframes, multi-coloured floor-tiles from Faenza, coffered ceilings and tapestries. Next to the King's bedroom there was the library containing the King's world famous collecton, the Bibliotheca Corviniana. On one of the vaults in the library, the starry sky was painted in the exact constellation of planets at the moment of the ruler's birth. Renaissance emblems adorned the gilt wooden ceiling of the nearby throne hall. The wing overlooking the Danube housed the richly equipped observatorium. A Marble Courtyard on the western side served as a place of repose. A huge row of steps was built between the Water-town and the Castle; the waters from the springs on Szabadság Hill were conducted to the Castle.

The medieval residence of Hungarian kings saw stormy centuries in the following periods. Turks demolished it, fires devastated it, the walls were hit by cannonballs, and the treasuries ransacked. The little that remained, was lost during the recapture of Buda in 1686.

The Baroque age again witnessed an upswing in development. A huge building complex was erected in the middle of the 18th century for Queen Maria Theresa. This palace — for a time the home of the university of Buda — later became the residence of the Hungarian governors, and fell victim to the flames of the 1848 War of Independence.

From the 1867 Compromise with the Habsburgs until 1945, Buda Castle was again turned into an administrative district, the palace serving first as residence of King and Emperor Francis Joseph I on his visits from Vienna, and later as of the Governor.

The Palace was grandly rebuilt at the turn of the century on the occasion of the millennial celebrations, only to be completely burnt out during World War II.

This last devastation, though, seems, paradoxically to have had a saving grace. In the course of rubble clearance, rebuilding acivity was aimed at the conservation of Gothic and Renaissance remains that came to light. The Castle District we see today is richly variegated with bastions, façades, conserved foundations of old buildings, statues and architectural decorations.

In the southern wing which houses the Budapest Histo-

8. The northern entrace with the equestrian statue of Eugene de Savoy in the background (József Róna, 1900)

ry Museum, visitors can see reconstructed bastions and walls, the Barbican and the Great Rondella. These belonged to the defence system of the medieval castle. The garden is graced with the favourite plants of one-time ladies of the court: roses, lemon trees, figtrees, pomegranate, lilies and lilies-of-the-valley.

Statues adorn the huge courtyards of the Palace, the best known representing *King Matthias on a hunt.* Opposite stands the statue of a *Hungarian csikós.* On the Danube side a monument to *Eugene of Savoy,* famous for defeating the Turks, can be seen. Buda Castle, the former royal residence, a centre for centuries of the country's administration, is today a tourist attraction and also a cultural centre, with architectural relics well-conserved. The monumental building complex houses three great museums and the National Library.

9. The inner courtyard of Buda Castle

10. The Matthias fountain (Alajos Stróbl, 1904)

11. *The Jánosrét Master: right wing of the St Nicolas altar, with scenes from the saint's life (around 1476)*

13. Madonna from Toporc (around 1420-1430)

THE HUNGARIAN NATIONAL GALLERY

This Gallery houses works by Hungarian artists or by artists resident in Hungary from the times of the founding of the state up to the present day.

The Old Gallery exhibits statues and panel paintings by medieval, Renaissance and Baroque artists. The Renaissance lapidary also forms part of the collection. In the former throne hall gilt Gothic winged altars can be seen.

The 19th-20th century collection gives a representative picture of the creation and development of Hungarian national art. The best-known masters of the age were *Károly Markó, Mihály Munkácsy, Bertalan Székely, Károly Lotz, Gyula Benczúr* and *Pál Szinyei Merse.*

The Modern Collection displays contemporary paintings, sculpture and medals. Among the rich collection the unique and hallucinatory visions of *Tivadar Csontváry Kosztka* deserve special mention.

Temporary shows exhibit foreign works of art too, such as those by *Salvador Dali* or from the Ludwig collection.

12. The collection of medieval winged altars

14. Károly
Markó
the Elder:
Landscape
in Appeggi
(1848)

15. Mihály
Munkácsy:
Storm in the
Puszta (1867)

16. Gyula
Benczúr: The
Christening of
Vajk (1875)

17. Tivadar Csontváry Kosztka: Ruins of the Greek Theatre at Taormina (1904-1905)

THE NATIONAL SZÉCHÉNYI LIBRARY

The name comes from Count Ferenc Széchényi who, in 1802, donated his rich collection to the nation. The aim of the library is to collect all publications related to Hungary. The library now boasts more then five million items.

The manuscript department preserves Hungary's oldest textual relic, the Funeral Oration, which came down to us in a late 12th century codex, called Pray-codex. The *Illuminated Chronicle,* written in Latin around 1360, relates Hungarian history up to the age of Charles Robert.

In the Old Prints Department we can find, among 7 100 incunabula, a copy of Gutenberg's 42 verse Bible.

Especially beautiful are the 32 codices from King Matthias' *Bibliotheca Corviniana.* Sixteen of these were given back to Hungary in the last century as a gift from the Turkish Sultan. From the 2000—2500 priceless volumes of the Bibliotheca, some 170 today are known throughout the world. Italian Humanist scholars helped the King to acquire these rarities, and artists in Buda workshops copied them and contributed to their richly ornamented binding.

18. Codices in the Library

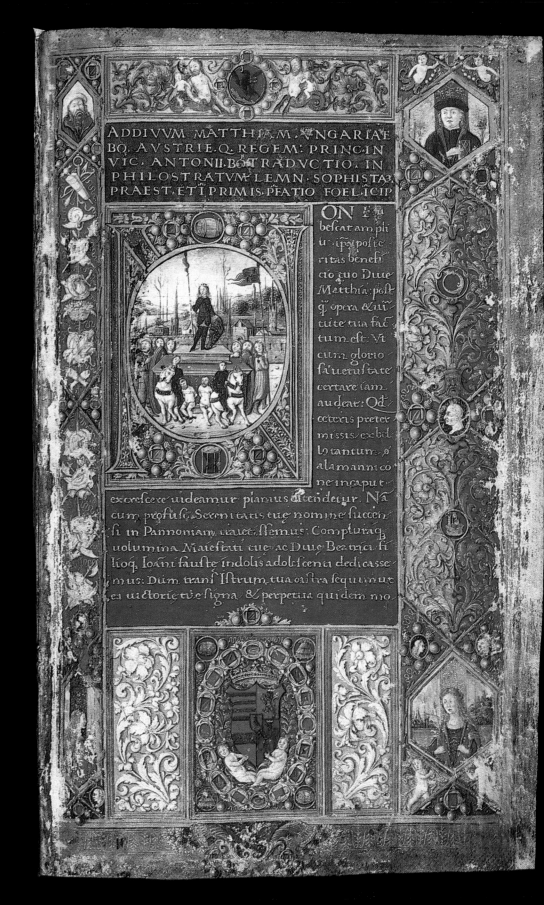

*19. The Philostratus
Codex from the
Bibliotheca
Corviniana.
On the tittle page
János Corvinus, son of
King Matthias at the
head of a triumphal
march to Vienna
(1487-1490)*

20. *Fragment of a statue from the period of King Sigismund*

21. *Matthias Corvinus — a relief by a Lombard master (1485-1490)*

22. *The crypt in the medieval royal castle*

THE BUDAPEST HISTORY MUSEUM

This museum exhibits items relating to archaeology, economical history and cultural history which concern the peoples that have lived in the territory of present-day Budapest. In a painstakingly reconstructed historical setting it is medieval relics which have found their proper place. The various phases of the construction of the palace are exhibited in huge halls.

In the Renaissance Hall superb marble fireplaces and doorframes, glazed stove-tiles decorated with the king's portrait, and Italian floor-tiles serve to illustrate the luxury of the royal court. The chapel named after St John of the Alms, still preserves an atmosphere of bygone devotion. In the centre stands a 15th century gilt winged altar.

Underneath, visitors can see the Albrecht-cellar, the icehouse and the former royal kitchen among others.

The objects displayed are mostly those of everyday life: pottery and glassware, mayolica, arms and armour, all attesting to the skills of past one-time artistans and craftsmen in Buda.

During reconstruction in the Castle, several years ago a lucky excavation brought to light a significant ensemble of statues from the Anjou (Angevin) period. With these, the medieval collection of the museum was turned into one of Europe's best Gothic galleries. The extraordinary beauty of the statues, displayed in the Knights' Hall of the Palace, amazed even specialists, and enchants the eye of contemporary visitors.

23. The fortifications of the medieval castle with the Mace Tower

24. Matthias Church (rebuilt by Frigyes Schulek, 1874-1896)

25. Mass in the Matthias Church

Objects in the treasury of Matthias Church:

26. Medieval winged altar from Felsőerdőfalva

27. Chalice from the 15th century

28. Monstrance from the 17th—18th century

THE CASTLE DISTRICT

From the Palace court a slight slope leads to Szentháromság (Holy Trinity) Square. It is a special feature that the city of Buda lies higher than the Palace itself.

The square is hallmarked by The Church of Our Lady, also known as *Matthias Church,* the reconstruction of which followed both the original form and the principles of Gothic architecture. It is one of the centres of both Catholic ecclesiastical life and of Hungarian history. King Matthias Corvinus, after whom the church is named, placed his coat-of-arms with the raven (*corvus* in Latin) on the Southern tower in 1470.

The church has since centuries been the site of many significant events of Hungarian history. It was here that Charles Robert was crowned in 1309, and kings of Hungary who were crowned in Székesfehérvár were introduced to the people of the capital. Within the walls of the church were the deceased rulers laid in state, royal weddings held, military banners and captured war emblems kept. Legend has it that it was also here, in this church, that the first bells were tolling at noon to commemorate the victory over the Ottoman army, a habit that has ever been in custom in the Christian world after the victory at Nándorfehérvár (today's Belgrade) in 1456.

Paintings and stained glass windows of the interior are like a picture book to recall significant events of the history of Hungary.

The church has for centuries also been the centre of ecclesiastical music in Hungary. It saw the première of Franz Liszt's *Coronation Mass* in 1867, and that of Zoltán Kodály's *Te Deum of Buda Castle* in 1936.

Holy Trinity Square was the centre of medieval Buda, with the marketplace and the Town Hall. In its centre now stands an ornamented plague coloumn erected in the 18th century after a severe epidemic.

Behind Matthias Church is the Fishermen's Bastion, one of the most famous lookout places of the capital. The neo-Romanesque building complex got its name after the guild of the fishermen who, according to tradition, had their defence bastion in this place. The row of arcades reminding of Romanesque cloisters encircles the equestrian statue of King (Saint) Stephen I, founder of the Hungarian state.

Nearby *Hilton Hotel* is one of the most elegant hotels in Budapest. It stands in the place of a medieval church

30—32. Holy Trinity Square and the Fishermen's Bastion

and monastery of the Dominican Order, the remains of the walls are uniquely combined with the contemporary building. In the inner courtyard open air concerts are held.

The contemporary network of streets in the Castle District follows the medieval structure of the district. Here, in this densely inhabited area stood the houses of the rich burghers and aristocracy, as well as inns and shops. Big inner courtyards and Gothic *sedilia* in the gateways tell us about the busy life of bygone centuries. Street-bridges joining two houses once so common, were demolished, now only one of them can be seen in Balta köz.

Tourists are recommended to go and see the closed inner courtyards with their quaint old gardens, medieval remains, vaulted windows.

33. A complex of architectural relics and the Hilton Hotel

34. A performance in the courtyard of Hilton Hotel ▷

Beneath the Castle District there was another world — that of cellars. These were used as wine and food stores — today they hide fancy restaurants, elegant shops, and one of them houses a wax museum.

The Castle District in Buda, with its Gothic, Renaissance, Baroque and more recent, historicizing buildings is, as a complex deserving attention, under the protection of UNESCO.

35. Medieval Houses at Tárnok Street. The fresco is from the early 1500s

◁ *36—37. A Baroque and a medieval gateway with sedilia*

38—40. Ornamented houses in the Castle District

◁ 41. The Pharmacy Museum
in the building of the
18th century 'Golden Eagle'
Pharmacy

42. Lion holding a coat of arms
on the façade
of No 13 Úri Street

43. Detail of Országház Street
with medieval consoles
on the façades

48. The cable
railway,
a reconstructed
industrial relic

49. The Chain ▷
Bridge as seen
from the tunnel in
Buda

50. *Elizabeth Bridge with the Danube bank in Pest*

THE DANUBE BANK

Travelling down on the cable railway, we can see the *Chain Bridge*, the first permanent bridge to span the Danube, the construction of which was initiated by Count István Széchenyi, 'the greatest Hungarian'. The bridge has become the symbol of a period, the Reform Era. It was planned by the Englishman Tierney Clark and built by his namesake, the Scotsman, later to settle in Hungary, Adam Clark. A direct continuation of the bridge is the *Tunnel*, which leads under Castle Hill.

The graceful *Elizabeth Bridge* is on the site of a river crossing that existed several thousand years ago. It was named after Queen Elizabeth, wife of Emperor Francis

Joseph I. For a long time it was the longest-span suspension bridge in the world. In 1945, during the siege of the city, the bridge was so severely damaged that reconstruction seemed impossible. In its new form it was rebuilt as a cable bridge. Both its forms were the creation of Hungarian architects. Near its Buda end, in a nice little park stands the statue of Queen Elizabeth.

The valley that lies between the Castle and Gellért Hill is called Tabán, whose parks are a favourite area for recreation and sport. In the bushes that grow on the slopes of Gellért Hill we can behold the *St Gerard (Gellért) monument.* The bishop saint was the tutor of the son of Hungary's first King, Stephen I, and it was from the spot where

51. *The Castle Garden Bazaar (Miklós Ybl, 1875-1882)*

the monument now stands that he was thrown into the Danube by the pagans. The waterfall underneath is especially beautiful when lit up in the evenings.

Further to the south is *Liberty Bridge* (the former Francis Joseph Bridge). The bridge is decorated by the *turul,* imaginary birds of prey that were a totemic animal of the ancient Hungarians.

52. *Statue of St Gerard with the waterfall*
(Gyula Jankovits, 1904)

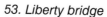

53. Liberty bridge

BUDAPEST — A HEALTH RESORT

Budapest is a world-famous health resort. In the depths stretches a North-South tectonic breakage line, thanks to which Buda and its environs are rich in medicinal thermal springs. These are utilized by hospitals in Buda and by swimming pools and thermal hotels on both sides of the river and on Margaret Island. One of them is the elegant *Gellért Spa Hotel,* with its white limestone walls, huge glass surfaces, big halls and fine sculptures.

The advantage of thermal waters was already known to prehistoric man. In the Roman period, and later, during the Middle Ages and the Turkish occupation, bathing and taking the waters was very popular in Buda and remains so today.

54-56. General view and details of the Gellért Baths — the outdoor swimming pool and the effervescent water bath (Ármin Hegedűs, Artúr Sebestyén, Izidor Stark, 1912—1918)

57-58. Király Bath . . . and its pool from the Turkish period

Turkish rule lasted for 150 years, and few buildings, with the exception of mosques and baths, remained. The thermal waters in Buda were extremely popular with Turkish Pashas stationed here. With reverence to Allah, they supported the construction of baths with rich donations. The famous Pasha Sokollu Mustapha ruled between 1566 and 1578 in Buda and had the *Király Baths* built. Later Baroque and neo-Classical additions were made to the building. Near the baths stands the small *Florian Chapel,* the Greek Catholic parish church of Buda.

BATTHYÁNY SQUARE AND ST ANNE'S CHURCH

Batthyány Square is the centre of the Watertown, the district stretching below Castle Hill. The square's former name was the Upper Marketplace, because from 1696 on — after the expulsion of the Turks — the annual fairs were held here. The square was given its present name in 1905, after the Prime Minister of the first responsible Hungarian Government, who died a martyr's death in 1848.

The Roman Catholic parish *Church of St Anne,* one of the finest examples of high Baroque style, stands in the Watertown on the Danube bank. Its twin towers can be seen from afar. The vaulted sill of its main entrance is decorated with the allegorical statues of Faith, Hope and Love, while in the middle stands the statue of St Anne with her Infant Mary. Above these the Buda coat of arms can be seen. The statues decorating the façade are the work of Antal Eberhardt, from 1759—60.

The interior of the church is no less rewarding — the richly adorned main altar is the work of Károly Bebo, a leading church architect in the 18th century. The altar represents St Anne presenting her daughter in the church at Jerusalem. The church has a fine Baroque organ, formerly in the church of the Carmelites in Buda Castle.

The Angelica café which occupies the ground floor of the parish building hosts literary evenings. On the northern side of the square stands the church, hospital and nunnery of the Elizabethan order. The building complex which dates from 1731—37 is now a home for the aged.

Next to it stands the statue of the great Hungarian poet, Ferenc Kölcsey.

Batthyány Square offers several sights of historical and artistic significance, such as the former White Cross Inn, with its Rococo facade, where theatrical performances and balls were held in the 18th century. Among the guests of the small palace was Emperor Joseph II, 'the hatted king'.

Today the square is one of the busiest points in Buda, and one of the meeting points of hikers starting out for the Buda mountains.

59-60. St Anne's Church and the organ
(Kristóf Hamon, Máté Nepauer; around 1740)

61. Umbrellas — a composition by Imre Varga

MAIN SQUARE (FŐ TÉR)

This small square is a little island left from Old Buda built on Roman wall remains. With its quaint, one-storey houses it has long preserved the quiet atmosphere of bygone centuries. This is enhanced by a composition by Imre Varga, a contemporaray Hungarian sculptor. Guests should visit restaurants and wine cellars, while outdoor fairs offer arts and crafts ware.

62. A period horse cart in the Main Square at Óbuda

63. Roman ruins and the Museum in Aquincum

AQUINCUM

Beside the ruins of the civilian and military amphitheatres, baths, villas and other buildings, the garden of ruins around *Aquincum Museum* indicates how vivid life was here some 2000 years ago. Although little has been left from the grandiose Palace of Emperor Hadrian on nearby Shipyard Island, excavations have brought to light precious objects, frescoes, mosaics and a unique water organ, all telling of the high level of culture of both the civilian

64. Roman mosaic floor depicting the story of Hercules from the villa in Meggyfa Street

and the military towns in one-time Pannonia. Near the garden of ruins is the reconstruction of a small section of the one-time Roman aquaeduct which supplied water to the twin cities.

This section of the Danube bank is called *Római part,* and is a favourite recreation area with townspeople. One of the biggest campsites in the city can also be found here, together with swimming pools, boathouses and fish restaurants.

THE CASTLE MUSEUM AT NAGYTÉTÉNY

The Baroque mansion built on Roman and medieval foundations houses a rich collection of European and Hungarian furniture. A special place is occupied by 18th-century French and English pieces. The latter deserves special mention for being so much different from those on the Continent. The history of Hungarian furniture is represented from the Gothic period on, the bulk however is from the Baroque period.

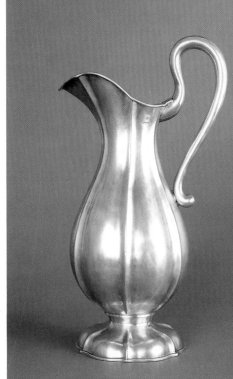

◁ *65. The Castle Museum at Nagytétény*

66. A file from the collection of the Kiscell Museum

67. A silver jug for handwashing by József Szentpétery, 19th century goldsmith

Beside nicely displayed pieces of furniture, carpets, stoves and other objects form a harmonic unity of interior decoration.

KISCELL MUSEUM

This museum is in the building of the former Trinitarian church and monastery built in the 18th century. The complex was donated by will to the capital in 1935.

From the material exhibited, special mention must be made of the graphic collection, displaying representations of the cityscape from the late 15th century up to our days; portaraits of prominent figures of Hungarian public life, fashion and genre pictures. The town history material offers works of applied art — furniture, clothing, clocks, other *objets d'art* such as porcelain, glassware and silverware. In the nearby church temporary art shows are organized in the summer season.

MARGARET ISLAND

This island, under the reign of the first kings of the Árpád dynasty, was a royal park of game, called the Island of Hare. Its present-day name comes from the daughter of King Béla IV, Princess Margaret, who lived and died here in a nunnery.

Margaret Island nowadays is a recreation area with limited traffic and protected flora. The area consists mostly of paths flanked by old trees, of rose gardens and lawns, there are two spa hotels, the Thermal and Ramada Grand Hotel and several sport grounds, an open-air cinema and a theatre and an old water tower on the island. Peacocks walk freely in the lawn and wild ducks nest on the water.

Grand Hotel which now belongs to the Ramada chain is visited mostly by rulers, politicians and famous people both as private and official guests.

In the summer period the hotel can also be reached by boat and water taxi.

Margaret Island is a favourite place with townspeople, families with small children and the old, if they long for nature in a place easy of access.

69. *The park*

70. *The pond*

71. *The Water Tower*

72. *Waterfall*

73—74. The Ramada Spa Hotel and the terrace

75. Bathers at the Thermal Hotel on Margaret Island

76. Performance in the outdoor theatre on the Island

THE PARLIAMENT BUILDING

On the left bank of the Danube stands the neo-Gothic Parliament building, an imposing example of *fin-de-siècle,* historicizing, eclectic architecture. Both its outer form and its inside reflect the general taste of the millennial festivities of 1896, when Hungary celebrated the one-thousandth anniversary of the Magyar Conquest. The architect had been influenced by neo-Gothic Houses of Parliament in London, and by the Cathedral in Cologne. The Parliament has been the centre of Hungarian administration since 1904. The Gothic style building has a Baroque spatial effect. In the hall under the stellar vault of the dome receptions and ceremonies are held. The main staircase also leads from here. The dome unites the two wings of the building. The carefully executed unique decoration of the Parliament was designed by Imre Steindl; the architect's plans were realized by the best decorative artists, painters and sculptors of the age. 'I used the flowers of Hungary's fields, meadows and forests in a stylized form', the architect wrote. The outside of the building is decorated with 90 statues representing the great figures of Hungarian history. The halls are adorned with frescoes depicting historical scenes from the Magyars' beginnings till the coronation in 1867.

77. The façade on the Danube side of the Parliament (Imre Steindl 1904)

78. The cupola of the Parliament

79. Decorations in the House of Representatives

80. The ornamental staircase

81. A king's statue

THE ETHNOGRAPHICAL MUSEUM AND THE NATIONAL BANK OF HUNGARY

The collection and the scientific workshop in this museum are among the oldest of their kind in the world. The museum was founded by Antal Reguly. Although the museum principally collects items of Hungarian origin, the fine collections of ceramics and textile contain pieces from all over Europe. The department of folk music has the oldest material found by Béla Bartók and Zoltán Kodály.

Hungary never had any colonies. Researchers or members of the aristocracy have, however, donated many exotic pieces to the museum.

The neo-Classical, eclectic building, constructed in the millennary period to the plans of Alajos Hauszmann, was originally the building of the Royal Supreme Court. With its huge bloc with four facades it resembles the ominous building of the Berlin Reichstag. The statues decorating it point to its original function — the allegoric figures represent the Law-maker, the Master of the Law, the Condemned, the Acquitted, the Public Prosecutor and the Defender. The frescoes of the ceiling in the great hall are the work of Károly Lotz.

The ensemble of the Museum, the Parliament, Kossuth Square and the streets leading up to it show despite later alterations all the marks of *fin-de-siècle* conscious town-planning.

82—83. Façade of the Ethnographical Museum and the entrance hall (Alajos Hauszmann, 1893—1896)

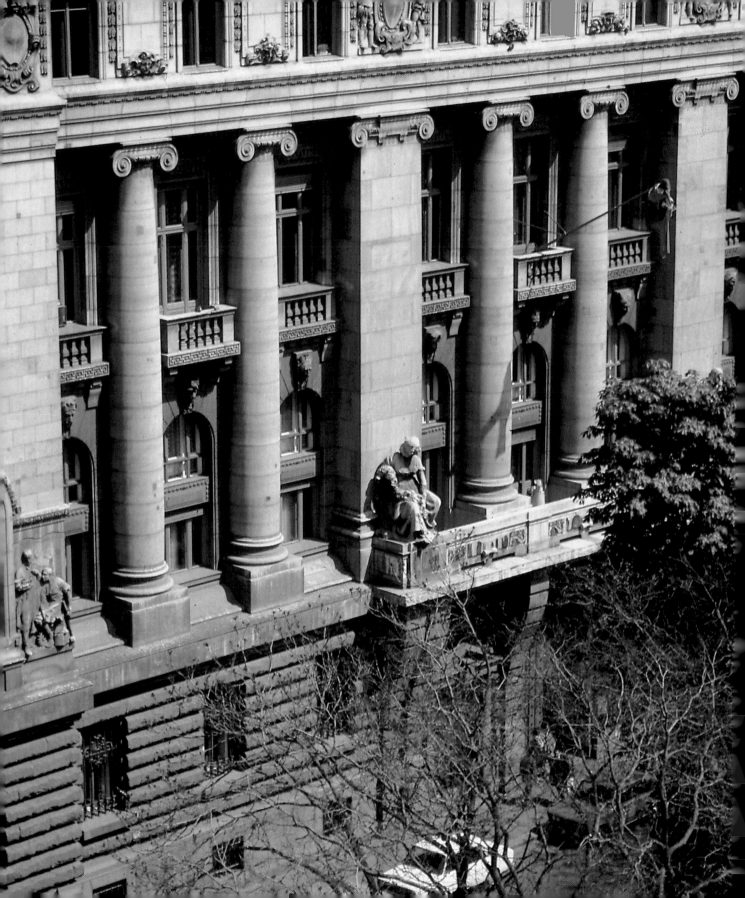

◁ *84. Façade of the National Bank of Hungary
(Ignác Alpár, 1905)*

85—86. Art nouveau details

87. The session hall of the Bank

Near the centre of administration, the Parliament, several other artistically formed and decorated buildings house important public institutions and offices.

One of them is the *National Bank of Hungary,* planned by the renowned specialist of bank architecture, Ignác Alpár.

The robust architecture, lavish decorations and the use of precious materials all point to the richness, reliability and dignity of banking activity. The interior decoration, according to the taste of the age, is a mixture of gradious Baroque and neo-Classicism, with *art nouveau* elements. The latter, usually more playful and light, seem in this context severe and dignified.

THE INNER CITY

The symbol of the historical Inner City of Pest is *Váci utca* (street). Metropolitan life is at its busiest here. Barefooted tourists stroll here alongside such public figures as Mrs Thatcher or Mikhail and Raisa Gorbachev. Elegant tourists mingle with the students of the nearby university. Visitors often say that Budapest is the Paris of Middle Europe — Váci utca is surely one of the reasons why. Banks and commercial buildings old and new, small boutiques and elegant department stores give way to small-windowed cafés. Most of the houses here have an inner courtyard and several entrances. Almost all architectural styles of the last two centuries can be found here, perfectly harmonised.

The line of the ornamentally covered street follows that of the medieval city walls. Chandeliers evoke a *fin-de-siècle* atmosphere. In the middle of the square named after him stands the white marble statue of the great Hungarian poet, *Mihály Vörösmarty*. In this square is the famous Gerbeaud pastry shop, the best-known in Budapest, once visited by Queen Elizabeth. The department store called *Luxus* was built at the turn of the century.

93. Christmas in Vörösmarty Square

94. Váci utca by night ▷

95—97. The Romantic façade and details of the Vigadó in Pest (Frigyes Feszl, 1859—1864)

98. The staircase with a fresco by Mór Than ▷

Street musicians and portrait artists, actors and other showmen amuse passers-by. The area, nevertheless, is not just a tourist attraction. In the mornings people rush to work here, during the day tourists stroll and gaze. At night, when the windows of the office buildings are already dark, restaurants, pastry-shops and shopwindows remain brightly alive.

On the Danube side, its back to the square, stands the *Vigadó,* the former Redoute. Built at the beginning of the 19th century, in the upswing of the Reform Era, it was a centre for art and entertainment. During the 1848—49 War of Independence, it housed the sessions of the 'rebellious' parliament, and was therefore demolished. The new building is the work of Frigyes Feszl. The Vigadó suffered severe damage during World War II, and is in its reconstructed form an exact copy of Frigyes Feszl's building. The most precious parts of the façade, reliefs with dancers, are the work of Károly Alexy.

99. The Pest Danube bank with the row of hotels

The Vigadó's walls witnessed many significant events of Budapest's musical life, concerts given by Franz Liszt and Brahms, as well as by Debussy or Pablo Casals. Elegant balls and other social events of the capital were also held here. Exhibitions, concerts and theatrical performances are still a great attraction.

The small square in front of the building, flanked by hotels, and a section of the upper embankment of the Danube is another favourite place of strollers. The fresh northwest wind from the Danube changes the air; from spring till autumn there are outdoor restaurants for those seeking refreshment after sightseeing. On the other side of the Danube, Castle Hill, Gellért Hill, the Buda mountains and the bridges offer a beautiful panorama.

In summer, near the row of hotels on the Pest side, stands a ship converted into a restaurant. The city can also be viewed from aboard ferry boats and water taxis.

At the Pest head of graceful Elizabeth Bridge, in *Feren-*

100. The terrace of the Hotel Duna Intercontinental

101. Dunakorzó

102. Pigeons on Vigadó Square

103. Interior of the Atrium Hyatt Hotel

ciek tere, are the twin buildings known as the *Klotild* palaces. Near the nothern one narrow, elegant *Kígyó Street* leads to Váci utca.

This area is the kernel of the city of Pest. Under the bridgehead Roman ruins evoke the time when, under the name Contra Aquincum, there stood here the left-bank fortress of the capital of Pannonia. Next to this stands the Inner City Parish Church which was built on foundations from the Árpádian era.

The *Paris Arcades,* a system of passages on the ground floor of the former Inner City Savings Bank, is a busy shopping centre with boutiques and cafés.

104. *Ferenciek tere*

105. *The Paris courtyard by night* ▷

ST STEPHEN'S CATHEDRAL (THE BASILICA)

St Stephen's is one of the main centres of the Catholic Church in Hungary. Its name refers to its ecclesiastical rank and not to its architectural structure. Begun by József Hild in the midde of the last century, its construction was completed by Miklós Ybl. The cupola is one of the characteristics of the city skyline. The interior is a rich collection of late 19th century Hungarian fine art. The mosaics, altarpieces ans statues are the work of Bertalan Székely, Károly Lotz, Gyula Benczúr, Árpád Feszty, Alajos Stróbl, and János Fadrusz. In the Basilica is kept the *Holy Dexter* of King Saint Stephen, founder of the Hungarian state, a relic both national and ecclesiastical.

The neo-Classic *Lutheran church in Deák Square* with

106—107. St Stephen's Cathedral (József Hild, Miklós Ybl, 1851—1905) and its sanctuary with the Carrara marble statue of St Stephen

its huge vaulted roof structure, was built by Mihály Pollack between 1799 and 1809. The designer, János Krausz planned a single great interior, an innovation among traditional forms of church architecture. The vaulted junction between the church and the school — now the *National Lutheran Museum* — served as a school at the beginning of the 19th century; Sándor Petőfi, the great Hungarian poet, studied here in the school-year 1833—34.

The *Serbian Orthodox church in Petőfi Square,* in the

*108. The Lutheran church in Deák Square
(Mihály Pollack, 1799-1809)*

*109. The Synagogue in Dohány Street
(Ludwig Förster, 1854—1859)*

Inner City of Pest, was built in the early 1700s in the Baroque style. The façade was later rebuilt by Miklós Ybl. The iconostasis is of great value, and is the work of the Serbian master Miklós Jankovich.

The *Synagogue in Dohány Street,* one of the largest in the world, is both a national relic and a treasure of the world Jewry. It was built in the middle of the last century in a consciously archaic Romantic-Eastern style. It is now being reconstructed with donations from all over the world, one of its main sponsors being Tony Curtis, who is of Hungarian origin. A side-building houses the *National Jewish Museum.*

*110. Iconostasis by Miklós Jankovich in the Greek
Orthodox Church in Petőfi Square (1791—1794)*

THE HUNGARIAN NATIONAL MUSEUM

This exceptionally beautiful building of Classical proportions is the work of Mihály Pollack (1839—1846). The tympanum above the neo-Classical main façade represents Pannonia, the patroness of the Sciences and Arts. The frescoes on the walls of the ceremonial staircase depict the history of Hungary from the migration from Asia up to 1848. The staircase leads to a domed hall where the Royal Crown and other coronation regalia are displayed. After World War II these items were taken to the US, but were later returned to Hungary. St Stephen's crown is not merely a royal jewel but is the symbol of the country's national independence.

The founder of the National Museum was Ferenc Széchényi. The Museum collects relics related to Hungary and its history from the Paleolithic age up to 1945. Three permanent exhibitions can be visited. The one entitled *The History of the Peoples of Hungary from the Paleolithic Age to the Magyar Conquest* displays historical relics of peoples that once lived in the territory of Hungary, and a collection of princely treasures from the Migration Period.

The exhibition entitled *The History of the Hungarian People from the Magyar Conquest to 1848* begins with a display of the jewels, attire and armour of the conquering

111. The Hungarian National Museum (Mihály Pollack, 1839—1846)

112. The ornamental staircase of the museum with frescoes by Károly Lotz and Mór Than

113. A looted Turkish tent and its interior in the museum

Magyars, then gives a picture of the various periods of the culture of Christianized Hungarians. Unique historical relics are to be found here. A true rarity is a *saddle* adorned with small bone plates made for King and Emperor Sigismund of Luxembourg, later Holy Roman Emperor. Only 20 such pieces are known to exist in the world. Further items worthy of interest are the *Turkish tent* looted from the enemy, relics of the *Thököly* and *Rákóczi* families, and various objects from the Reform Period and from the 1848 War of Independence. The treasury keeps fine works of goldsmithery, among them the *Monomachos crown* and the *Pálffy chalice*.

114. These furnishings belonged to Prince Ferenc Rákóczi II

115. The Holy Crown, symbol of Hungary's national independence, 11th—12th century

116. The Constantions Monomachos crown from Byzantium (1043), cloisonné enamel

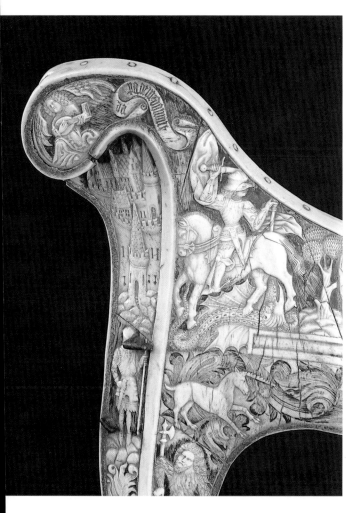

117. Detail of an ornamental bone saddle with the figure of a knight, from the Buda workshop of King Sigismund of Luxembourg (early 15th century)

The exhibition entitled *The Hungarian Coronation Regalia* displays, beside the crown, the sceptre, the orb, the sword and the coronation mantle.

The building itself is a relic of national history, as it was from here that the revolution in 1848 started. On its arriversary, the 15th of March, young people gather every year to pay tribute to the memory of the leaders, Lajos Kossuth and Sándor Petőfi.

118. Chalice of Miklós Pálffy (1589, gold and enamel)

THE MUSEUM OF APPLIED ARTS

At the intersection of the Great Boulevard and Üllői Street stands a building with a stange decoration and roof, it is the work of Ödön Lechner, the great master of Hungarian *art nouveau.* The stirking effect of the building is enhanced by the glazed roof-tiles from the Zsolnay factory.

In these decorations Hungarian motifs are mixed with Arabic and Islamic elements. This can be observed particularly in the galleries of the central hall, the architectural solution of which reflects the playfulness of *art nouveau.*

The *Museum of Applied Arts,* opened in 1896 — the year of the Millennial celebrations — is the third of its kind in Europe. The museum collects and studies objects of interior decoration and use. It has five departments, furniture, textile, goldsmithery, ceramics, and small collections.

In the *collection of ceramics* we find, beside works of art from the famous Hungarian Herend and Zsolnay factories, Italian Renaissance faience works, German stoneware from the 15th—18th centuries and porcelain from Meissen and Vienna. The *collection of textiles* boasts outstanding Flemish and French tapestries and fine eastern

119. The art nouveau Museum of Applied Arts (Ödön Lechner, Gyula Pártos, 1893—1896)

120. Characteristically Hungarian art nouveau ▷ elements in the museum

124. Christ's birth. Tapestry from Brussels
(around 1520)

121—122. Baroque jewels

123. The Szapolyai chalice, (gilt silver, from around 1520)

carpets. The *collection of goldsmith's works* has Renaissance and Baroque *objets d'art* both religious and secular in function, and the best pieces of Hungarian goldsmithery from the 17th—18th centuries. The most beautiful pieces of the *furniture collection* are displayed in the Castle Museum at Nagytétény. The *small collections* exhibit fans, ornamented books, toys and other everyday objects.

125. Kossuth Lajos Street

THE GREAT BOULEVARD (NAGYKÖRÚT)

Kossuth Lajos Street, an elegant shopping thoroughfare, starts at Elizabeth Bridge. From the predestrian underpass at Astoria, its continuation is called Rákóczi Street. Here a memorial tablet marks the place of the 15th century city wall and the Hatvani Gate.

This busy shopping street crosses the Great Boulevard at *Blaha Lujza Square,* a favourite meeting point for Budapest people. Here stood the National Theatre which was later demolished, with only a small stone to remind us of its former glory. The square takes its name from Lujza Blaha, one of the primadonnas of the theatre.

The city is at its busiest here on the Great Boulevard, which encircles the Inner City. From morning till night crowds of people pass in front of its theatres, night clubs, boutiques, stores and cafés. The Great Boulevard has a unified eclectic style unique in Europe. This unity of variety and *mélange* of different historical styles results in a harmonious appearance.

At Nyugati Square we find the *Western Railway Sta-*

*126. The Western Railway Station
(by the Gustave Eiffel Bureau, 1874—1877)*

127. Blaha Lujza Square

tion, whose iron laced glass hall is an architectural and industrial testament to the outstanding work of the Gustave Eiffel Bureau.

The avenue which begins at the middle section of Little Boulevard, *Andrássy street*, is at once the result and reflection of the *fin-de-siècle*. Beneath it runs the 'little metro', the underground which, when opened in 1896, was the first on the Continent.

THE OPERA HOUSE

A gem of the avenue is the *Opera House,* by Miklós Ybl — many prefer it to those of Vienna or Paris. The architect designed a façade which creates an illusion of it being a much larger building.

The two marble sphinxes on either side of the arcaded driveway are popular decorative elements of the capital. Near the entrance stand the Romantic-Realist limestone statues of two great Hungarian composers, Franz Liszt and Ferenc Erkel; on the façade smaller statues of famous composers and the Muses can be seen.

The architectural effect of the interior is enhanced by the masterly frecoes. The protagonists of the series adorning the vast surfaces are Apollo and Dionysios, two ancient Greek gods. Apollo represents the elevating, refining effect of music on the soul, Dionysios its unbridled force liberating the instincts. Other decorative artists of the interior were Mór Than, Bertalan Székely and Károly Lotz. One could say that the spectacle begins before the performance.

The Opera House is an important centre of musical life in Hungary, and the luminaries among Europe's artists have performed here during the last hundred years.

128. The Opera House
(Miklós Ybl, 1880—1884)

129. The auditorium of the
Opera House

130. The ornamental
staircase ▷

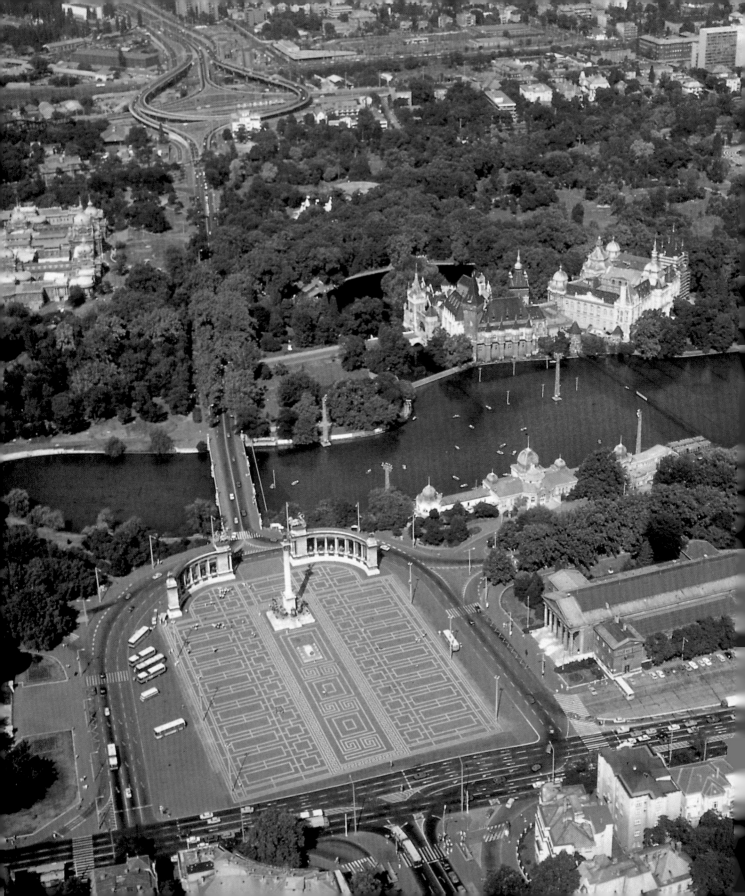

HEROES' SQUARE (HŐSÖK TERE)

Andrássy street, flanked by eclectic palaces, villas and trees leads up to *Heroes' Square*, with the *Millennial Monument*. In the centre of the semicircular colonnade rises the figure of the Archangel Gabriel on a high coloumn. This statue won a Paris Grand Prix in 1900 for its sculptor, György Zala. Under the column stand the equestrian figures of the seven Magyar conquering chieftains. Between the columns stand the statues of Hungarian kings and other outstanding historical personalities.

In the centre of the square is the marble memorial stone to Hungarian heroes, and wreaths are laid here on national holidays and on the occassion of high diplomatic visits. On the right stands the *Art Gallery*, the largest exhibition hall in the capital, and on the left, the *Museum of Fine Arts*.

◁ 131. Heroes' Square with the pond in City Park

132. The façade of the Art Gallery

133. The Millennial Monument in Heroes' Square

THE MUSEUM OF FINE ARTS

This museum houses the country's richest collection of European art and sculpture. The kernel of the collection was the former Esterházy Picture Gallery, purchased by the state in 1870. One of the main attractions of the Museum is Raphael's painting *'Portrait of a Youth'*, rescued after a notorious robbery. El Greco's canvases are among the best-known pictures in the Museum. The glowing colours against a dark background and the fantastically elongated forms intrigue the eye. The reproduction included in this book is of *'Christ on the Mount of Olives'*. In its one hundred and fifty years of existence the Museum has become one of the most valuable collections in Middle Europe, with pictures by Correggio, Veronese, Rembrandt, Titian, Zurbarán, Lorenzo Lotto, Brueghel the Elder, Goya, Delacroix, Cézanne, and others. The quantities of graphic material and the Egyptian and ancient collections are also worth mentioning.

134. The Museum of Fine Arts (Albert Schickedanz, Fülöp Herzog, 1906)

135. Portrait of a Youth (around 1504) by Raphael

136. Christ on the Cross by Memling

137. Mary with Her Child and an Angel (around 1520) by Correggio (Antonio Allegri)

138. Portrait of Doge Marcantonio Trevisani (after 1533) by Titian

139. Christ on the Mount of Olives by El Greco (Domenico Theotocopuli)

◁ 140. Girl with a Jug
by Francisco de Goya
(around 1810)

141. Horse Frightened by
Lightning (1824) by
Eugène Delacroix

142. Barges (1886) by
Claude Monet

THE CITY PARK (VÁROSLIGET)

Behind Hősök tere lies *City Park.* It has an area of around one square kilometre and offers entertainment, recreation and various sights. Its pond is an artifical skating rink in winter. On the small island stands *Vajdahunyad Castle,* built for the Millennial festivities. It is a fantastic mixture of different styles of architecture; its parts are copies of famous buildings from Hungary's historical and architectural past. Perhaps the best known is the castle of Vajda-hunyad (today Hunedoara, Rumania) hence the name of the whole building complex. The mock-castle houses the *Agricultural Museum* with a rich hunting exhibition.

The other imposing building in City Park is the *Széchenyi Baths.* At the edge of the park we wind the *Zoo,* the *Fun Fair,* the *Municipal Circus* and the famous *Gundel Restaurant.* On the right hand side of City Park are the *People's Stadium,* built in the 1950s, and *Petőfi Hall,* a recreation centre.

143. *Vajdahunyad Castle (Museum of Agriculture)*

144. *Autumn in the City Park* ▷

Now the moment has come to say goodbye to you. If your time with us has been memorable, if our artistic treasures or the sights of our city have delighted you, if you have spent a pleasant evening in one of our theatres, night clubs or casinos, if you have tasted and enjoyed the specialities of Hungarian cuisine — then Budapest looks forward to greeting you again.

145. Chance and charm . . . rendez-vous in Casino Budapest

147. The Hungária restaurant on the Great Boulevard

146. Maxim's night club

148. The Apotheosis of Hungaria on the façade of a house in the Inner City (Miksa Róth, 1906)

TOURIST INFORMATION

ON HUNGARY IN GENERAL

The Hungarian Republic lies in the heart of Europe, at the middle flow of the Rivers Danube and Tisza, in the Carpathian Basin. Its area covers 93,036 sq. kms (35,919 mq. mi), which makes it the 18th largest country in Europe.

Hungary can be divided into the following parts: Transdanubia in the west, where hilly regions alternate with plains; the Great Plain, which occupies the eastern and southeastern part; and the Northern Mountain Range. The climate is moderately continental, precipitation varies according to region.

All waters of the country belong to the catchment area of the Danube, the largest river of Middle Europe. With its 600 registered thermal springs, Hungary also abounds in medicinal and thermal waters. In minerals, though, the country is rather poor.

Hungary has 10.6 million inhabitants, of which 2 million live in the capital, Budapest. Regarding the density of population—114 per sq. km—the country ranks among the first ones in the world. There are also about 4 to 4.5 million Hungarians living as national minorities in the neighbouring countries.

Hungary is a republic. The national colours are red, white and green. The main organ of power is the Parliament. Legislation also belongs to the Parliament. The bases of legislation are outlined in the Constitution, which lists the rights of the citizens in detail. One of the basic tenets is: "The Hungarian Republic respects human rights". The Constitution ensures the liberty of conscience.

The most outstanding figures of Hungarian science made their mark as scholars in the fields of mathematics, cybernetics, physics, biology and economy. Among these are Nobel Prize winners Albert Szent-Györgyi (1937, physiology), György He-vesi (1943, chemistry), György Békésy (1961, physiology) and Dénes Gábor (1971, physics).

Although Hungary's musical traditions go back many centuries, it was Franz Liszt who put her on the map of European musical life. The turning point, however, came in the 20th century with the works of Béla Bartók and Zoltán Kodály. Hungarian conductors have also done their part in popularizing Hungary—Antal Doráti, Eugene Ormándy, Sir George Solti, György Széll, Frigyes Reiner, Ádám Medveczky, Ádám Fischer among them. The best known solo performers are József Szigeti, Zoltán Kocsis, Dezső Ránki and András Schiff. The operettas of Imre Kálmán and Ferenc Lehár are performed all over the world for those who like 19th century atmosphere and light melodies.

Literature in the Hungarian vernacular was hindered by the common use of Latin. The appearance of the ideals of the French Enlightenment had a stirring effect on literature, a high point of which was reached by the lyric poetry of Sándor Petőfi. The best known among Hungarian authors is Ferenc Molnár, whose plays like 'Liliom' and 'The Guardsman' are revived again and again on the major stages of the world.

The development of fine arts in Hungary was defined by the stormy history of the country. It was only in the 19th century that true national art was born, the best-known masters are Mihály Munkácsy, Bertalan Székely, Károly Lotz and Viktor Madarász.

Though influenced by European taste, Hungarian cuisine has over the centuries preserved its special flavours. Hungary is also famous for its fruits. Last but not least, the tasty dry and sweet wines of Hungary—Tokay Aszú, Badacsony Riesling, and Szürkebarát deserve special mention.

SIGHTS TO SEE

In Hungary, museums, memorial houses, etc. are usually open from Tuesdays to Sundays, between 10 a.m. and 6 p.m. They can be visited on state and church holidays as well, but are closed the day after. On January 1, December 26 and Easter Monday all museums are closed.

In the following list the builder or decorator of a building and the date of construction or major reconstruction is given in brackets. *Tér* means square, *utca* is street, *út* is avenue.

BUDA

THE CASTLE DISTRICT

Bécsi kapu tér
— Lutheran church (19th c.).
Kapisztrán tér
— Tower and ruins of the former Mary Magdalene Church (13—15th c.)
— Institute and Museum of Military History, house No. 4.
Tóth Árpád sétány
— Zsolnay ornamental well.
Úri utca
— Several medieval houses with Gothic parts, sedilia in the gateways, nice inner courtyards. Houses Nos 31, 32, 38 and 40.
— Castle Caves. Labyrinth under Buda Castle, house No. 9.
— The building of the former Parliament, earlier church and cloister of the Poor Clares, house No. 49.
— Former Franciscan monastery (today it houses institutions of the Hungarian Academy of Sciences), house No. 53.
Szentháromság utca
— Ruszwurm pastry-shop (1830), house No. 7.
— Old Town Hall (V. Ceresola, M. Nepauer, 1692—1774), house No. 2.
Szentháromság tér
— Statue of the Holy Trinity (1712—13)
— Church of Our Lady (Matthias Church) (13—15th c., reconstructed by Frigyes Schulek, 1874—96)
— Fishermen's Bastion (Frigyes Schulek, 1895—1902)
— Equestrian statue of King Saint Stephen (Alajos Stróbl, 1893—1906).
Hess András tér
— Hilton Hotel (Béla Pintér, János Sedlmayer, 1976). Ruins of the former Dominican monastery (13—15th c.) now are part of the building. House No. 1—3.
Fortuna utca
— Museum of Catering and Trade

Dísz tér
— The former Batthyány palace (J. Giessl 1744—1748) house No. 3.
— Medieval sedilia in the gateways, houses Nos 4, 5.
Táncsics Mihály utca
— Musical History Museum. Music life and instruments in Hungary. The former lodgings of Beethoven (M. Nepauer, 1750—1769) house No. 7.
— Medieval Jewish synagogue (15th century) House No. 26.
— The former Zichy palace with the ruins of a 15th century synagogue in the courtyard. House No. 21—23.
Tárnok utca
— 'Golden Eagle' Pharmacy Museum, house No. 18.
Színház utca
— Várszínház (Castle Theatre) (rebuilt from the former church of the Carmelites by Farkas Kempelen and Kristóf Hikisch, 1787) house No. 1—3.

BUDA CASTLE

The former royal castle. Enlarged between 1896 and 1903 by Miklós Ybl and Alajos Hauszmann. Ruins from the 13—15th c. under the present-day level.
— Museum of the Recent History of Hungary (Buda Castle, Building 'A').
— Hungarian National Gallery (Buda Castle, Buildings 'B', 'C' and 'D'). Late Renaissance and Baroque art, 1550—1800. Late-Gothic winged altars, medieval collection of stonework finds, Gothic wooden carvings and panel paintings, 14—15th c., 19th c. Hungarian painting. Works by Mihály Munkácsy, László Paál, Pál Szinyei Merse. 20th c. painting and sculpture. Hungarian art in the 11th—20th c.
— Budapest History Museum (Buda Castle, Building 'E'). Archeological excavations in Budapest. Two millennia of Budapest. Buda Castle in the Middle Ages, Gothic statues.
— National Széchényi Library, temporary exhibitions.

WATERTOWN

Fő utca
— Király Bath (Turkish, rebuilt by Mátyás Schmidt 1826) house No. 82—86
— St Francis' Church of the former Elizabethan nuns (Jakab Hans, 1731—1741) Baroque interior from 1777
Batthyány tér
— St Anne's Parish Church (Kristóf and Mátyás Hamon, Máté Nepauer, 1740—1755)
— Rococo house, the former White Cross Inn, house No. 4

Clark Ádám tér
- The 0 kilometre stone (Miklós Borsos)
- Cable railway, a reconstructed industrial relic
- Castle Garden Kiosk (Miklós Ybl, 1874—1879)
- Castle Garden Bazaar (Miklós Ybl, 1875—1882), opposite the statue of the architect (Ede Mayer, 1869)

MARGARET BRIDGE AND ENVIRONS

- The *turbe* (tomb) of Gül Baba (1543—1570), 14 Mecset utca
- Franciscan church (M. Nepauer 1753—1770) and monastery (1723—1768), 23 Margit körút
- Ganz Ábrahám Foundry Museum, 15 Ganz utca

GELLÉRT HILL AND ENVIRONS

- Christiantown Roman Catholic Parish Church (Kristóf Hikisch, 1795—1797)
- St Katherine's Roman Catholic Parish Church in the Tabán district (Keresztély Obergruber, 1728—1736). 11 Attila utca
- Semmelweis Medical History Museum. The birthplace of Ignác Semmelweis, 'savior of the mothers', who discovered puerperal fever, 1 Apród utca
- Statue of Queen Elizabeth (György Zala) at the Buda head of Elizabeth Bridge
- Statue of St Gerard (Gyula Jankovits, 1904) and waterfall
- Citadel (Emánuel Zita, Ferenc Keszelik, 1850—1854) on the top of Gellért Hill
- 'Urania' observatorium open for the general public, 3/b Sánc utca
- Gellért Hotel and Medicinal Baths (Ármin Hegedűs, Artur Sebestyén, 1911—1918), 1 Szt Gellért tér
- Rudas Baths (Turkish, 1566) and drinking hall. 9 Döbrentei tér
- Rác Baths (Turkish, rebuilt in 1864—1874), 1 Hadnagy utca
- Drinking hall built into the bridgehead of Elizabeth Bridge
- Fathomless Pond (Feneketlen tó), Bartók Béla open-air theatre, Kosztolányi Dezső tér
- Sas Hill, nature conservation area

SOUTHERN BUDA

- Borkatakomba, a restaurant in a former system of cellars, Nagytétényi út
- The former Rudnyánszky castle (1720—1730), now the furniture department of the Museum of Applied Arts. Lapidarium, french gardens, period furniture and interior decoration, stoves. 9 Kastélymúzeum utca
- Rose show at Nagytétény

ÓBUDA

- Lukács Baths (late neo-Classic, 1893—1894) and drinking hall, 15—19 Frankel Leó út
- Császár Baths (neo-Classic, 1806, 1841—1846, József Hild) 31—33 Frankel Leó út
- Budapest Gallery. Permanent show of Imre Varga, contemporary Hungarian sculptor. 7 Laktanya utca
- Kiscell Museum. Former Trinitarin monastery and church (J. Entzenhoffer, 1744). Exhibitions displaying the history of Budapest; historical relics from the Turkish era to 1848; 20th century Hungarian art. 108 Kiscelli utca
- Former Zichy mansion (J.H. Jager and K. Bebo, 1746—1752). Exhibition hall, open air concerts in the courtyard during summer. 1 Fő tér
- Óbuda Silk Mill (József Tallher, 1785), an industrial relic. 46 Miklós utca
- Exhibition Hall of the Budapest Gallery (15th c., a Baroque reconstruction in the 18 th c.), 158 Lajos utca
- Roman military ampitheatre, Nagyszombat utca
- Thermae maiores. Ruins of a Roman military baths. Pedestrian underpass at Flórián tér
- Aquincum Museum, 139 Szentendrei út
- Hercules villa, 19—21 Meggyfa utca.

MARGARET ISLAND

- Monument erected for the 100th anniversary of the unification of Pest, Buda and Óbuda
- National Sports Swimming Pool (Alfréd Hajós, 1930)
- Palatinus Outdoor Pool (István Janáky, 1937)
- Water Tower (Szilárd Zielinszky, 1911)
- Ruins of the cloister of Dominican nuns (13—15th c.)
- 'Tomb' of St. Margaret
- Ruins of a Franciscan church and monastery (13th c.)
- Ruins of a Premonstratensian church and monastery (12th c.).

PEST

Március 15. tér
- Statue of Sándor Petőfi (Adolf Huszár, 1882)
- Greek Orthodox church (József Jung, 1794—1801), 2/b Petőfi tér
- Contra Aquincum (site of archeological excavations)
- Inner City Roman Catholic parish church (the oldest building in Budapest, 12th c.).

Ferenciek tere
- Paris courtyard (Ignác Alpár, 1914)
- Nereid Fountain (Mihály Feszl, Ferenc Uhrl).

— Franciscan (Roman Catholic) church (1727—1743; 1858—1863)
— University Library (Antal Szkalniczky and Henrik Koch Jr., 1832), house No. 10

Károlyi Mihály utca
— The former Károlyi palace (Anton Pius Riegl and József Hofrichter, 1832). Petőfi Literary Museum, house No. 16
— University church (András Mayerhoffer, 1722—1742), Egyetem tér.

Váci utca
— A promenande and shopping centre, Taverna Hotel, Pesti Theatre.

Vörösmarty tér
— Gerbaud's pastry shop
— Csontváry Art Gallery.

Martinelli tér
— Church of the Servites (Roman Catholic, 1725—1732, present facade: József Diescher, 1871)

Vigadó tér
— Vigadó Concert Hall (Redoute, Frigyes Feszl,1859—1864), concert hall and art gallery.

Városház utca
— Palace of the Invalides, now the Mayor's Office (F. Prati, J. Hölbing, 1727—1735, A.E. Martinelli)

Erzsébet tér and vicinity
— Lutheran church at Deák tér (Mihály Pollack, 1799—1809)
— National Lutheran Museum (1795), 4 Deák tér.

Bajcsy-Zsilinszky út
— St. Stephen's Cathedral (Basilica, József Hild, Miklós Ybl, József Kauser, 1851—1905), 1 Szent István tér.

Roosevelt tér
— Gresham Palace (Zsigmond Quittner and József Vágó, 1907)
— Hungarian Academy of Sciences (Friedrich August Stüler, 1862—1864).
— Statue of Count István Széchenyi (József Engel, 1880)
— Statue of Ferenc Deák (Adolf Huszár, 1887)

Kossuth Lajos tér
— Parliament building (Imre Steindl, 1884—1904)
— Ethnographical Museum (Alajos Hauszmann, 1896) 12 Kossuth tér.

Szabadság tér
— National Bank of Hungary (Ignác Alpár, 1905)
— Headquarters of the Hungarian Television (the former Stock Exchange building, Ignác Alpár, 1905).
— Underground Railway Museum (Underpass at Deák Square)
— The building of the former Postal Savings Bank (Ödön Lechner, 1899—1902)

Little Boulevard (Kiskörút)
— University of Economics (former Main Customs Office, Miklós Ybl, 1871—1874), 7—9 Fővám tér

— Hungarian National Museum (Mihály Pollack, 1837—1847), 14—16 Múzeum körút.
The history of the peoples of Hungary up to the Magyar Conquest. The history of Hungary from the Magyar Conquest to 1849. The coronation regalia of Hungary.
— Calvinist Church at Deák Square (J. Hofrichter 1816—1830, J. Hild, 1848)
— Synagogue and National Collection of Jewish Religion and Art (Ludwig Förster, 1854—1859), 2 Dohány utca
— Gallery of Art Collectors, 82 Dohány utca.

Great Boulevard (Nagykörút)
— Museum of Applied Arts (Ödön Lechner and Gyula Pártos, 1874—1877). Atrs and crafts, 33—37 Üllői út
— Western Railway Station (Bureau of G. Eiffel, W. A. de Serres, 1874—1877), 55 Teréz krt.

Andrássy út
Postal Museum, house No. 3
— Hungarian State Opera House (Miklós Ybl, 1875—1844)
— Liszt Ferenc Academy of Music (Flóris Korb, Kálmán Giergl, 1904—1907), 8 Liszt Ferenc tér
— Liszt Ferenc Memorial Museum and Research Centre, 35 Vörösmarty utca
— Hopp Ferenc Museum of East Asiatic Art, house No. 103
— Ráth György Museum (China Museum), 12 Városligeti fasor.

Hősök tere (Heroes' Square)
— Millennial monument (Albert Schickedanz, Fülöp Herzog, György Zala, 1896—1929)
— Museum of Fine Arts (Albert Schickedanz and Fülöp Herzog, 1900). The greatest art collection in Hungary. The departments are: Egyptian exhibition; Greek-Roman exhibition, Modern foreign sculpture and painting; Italian and Netherlandish painting, Flemish and Spanish painting; German, Austrian and English painting; Modern Foreign Gallery; Old foreign sculpture collection; Graphics collection.
— Art Gallery (Albert Schickedanz, Fülöp Herzog, 1895).

Városliget (City Park)
— Museum of Agriculture (Vajdahunyad Castle). The history of Hungarian agriculture, catte-breeding, hunting, fishing and nature conservation (Ignác Alpár,1896; 1904—1908)
— Municipal Zoo and Botanical Gardens, 6—12 Állatkerti út
— Fun Fair, 14—16 Állatkerti út
— Transport Museum. The history of Hungarian transport. 11 Városligeti krt.
— People's stadium, 3—5 Stefánia út.

OTHER SIGHTS

Caves
— Pálvölgy Cave, 162 Szépvölgyi út
— Szemlőhegy Cave, 35 Pusztaszeri út.

Nature conservation areas
— Budakeszi Game Park, game and flower rarities of Hungary
— Sashegy Nature Conservation Area.
Excursions to the Buda Hills
Buses start from Moszkva tér to the hills encircling Budapest.
— Cogwheel railway (Városmajor—Széchenyi Hill)
— Children's railway (Hűvösvölgy—Széchenyi Hill)
— Teleferic (Zugliget—János Hill).
Lookout towers
Gellért Hill, Buda Castle, Szabadság Hill, Normafa, Hármashatár Hill, János Hill, watertower on Margaret Island.

THE ENVIRONS OF BUDAPEST

Zsámbék
— Ruins of the former Premontratensian provostry (13th century, rebulit in 1475)
— Roman Catholic church (1749-1752, the pulpit is the work of Károly Bebo, 1754)
— Lamp museum

Ráckeve
— Castle of Prince Eugene of Savoy (J. L. Hildebrand, 1702)
— Greek Orthodox Serbian church (1487, rebuilt in the Baroque style)

Gödöllő
— The former Grassalkovich castle (András Mayerhoffer, 1744-1747)

Ócsa
— Calvinist church (frist half of the 13th century)

Fót
— Roman Catholic church (Miklós Ybl, 1845—1855)

THE DANUBE BEND

ESZTERGOM
— Primatial cathedral (Pál Hühnel, János Packh, József Hild, 1802—1869, with the Bakócz chapel, 1507, Szent István tér
— Cathedral Treasury
— Balassa Bálint Museum and Cathedral Library (József Hild, 1853), 28 Bajcsy-Zsilinszky út

— Primatial Palace and Christian Museum (József Lippert,1881—1882), 2 Berényi Zsigmond utca
— Castle, Castle Museum (late 12th c.) 1 Szent István tér.

SZENTENDRE
— Blagovestenska church (András Mayerhoffer, 1752), Fő tér
— Preobrazhenska church (1741—1746), Bogdányi út
— Roman Catholic parish church (14—15th c.; 18th c.) Várdomb
— Collection of Serbian Ecclesiastical Art. 5 Engels utca
— Barcsay Jenő Museum, 1 Dumtsa Jenő utca
— Czóbel Béla Museum, 1 Templom tér
— Ferenczy Károly Museum (former Greek Orthodox Serbian school, 1793), 6 Marx tér
— Kovács Margit Museum (former merchant's house, around 1750), 1 Vastag György utca
— Roman collection of stonework finds, 1 Dunakanyar körút
— Outdoor Ethnographical Museum (Skanzen), 10—18 Szabadság-forrás út.

VÁC
— Cathedral (Isidore Canevale, 1762—1770), Konstantin tér
— Bridge on the Gombás brook (Ignác Oracsek, 1753—1758, statues: József Bechert 1752; 1758—1759)
— Triumphal arch of Queen Maria Theresa (Isidore Canevale, 1764), Köztársaság utca
— Greek church, today a museum, 19 Március 15. tér
— Petzval József Collection of the History of Photography, 9 Tragor Ignác utca.

VÁCRÁTÓT
— Botanical Garden

VERŐCEMAROS
— Gorka Géza Museum of Ceramics, Verőce, 22 Szamos utca.

VISEGRÁD
— King Matthias Museum of the Hungarian National Museum, 41 Fő utca
— Solomon Tower (13th c.)
— Ruins of the royal castle (14—15th c.), 27—29 Fő utca
— Castle (water bastion 13th c., citadel 13th c.).

ZEBEGÉNY
— Szőnyi István Memorial Museum, 7 Dr. Bartóky J. utca.

TOURIST SERVICES, SPORTS, ENTERTAINMENT

SIGHTSEEING TOURS

Data given below might change. Information: TOURINFORM, Tel: 117-9800

BUDAPEST

Tourist offices organize sightseeing tours by motor-coach at least once a day (several times during the peak tourist season). The tours take approx. 3 hours.

For the tours listed below, tickets are sold at IBUSZ offices and hotel receptions, in some occasions at the site as well.

The Parliament Building

All the year round IBUSZ Travel Agency starts motorcoaches from Erzsébet tér, Budapest V.

Programme 1: Wednesdays and Fridays 10:30 a.m., between 1 May and 31 October also at 1:30 p.m.

Programme 2: Mondays 10:30 a.m.

Programme 1 also includes the Hungarian National Gallery, Programme 2, the Matthias Church.

Similar programs are also organized by the BUDAPEST TOURIST

Budapest city tour by motorcoach

The tour takes 3 hours, and includes Heroes square, the Millennial Monument, view from the Danube bank, the Parliament and other public buildings, Gellért Hill, Fishermen's Bastion, and Matthias Church in the Castle District. The programme ends with a soft drink at the Hilton Hotel in Buda.

Buses start from stops No. 13, 14, and 15 of the Central Bus Station at Erzsébet tér,

— all the year round daily at 10:00 a.m.

— in April and September daily at 10:00 a.m. and 2:00 p.m.

— 1 May—31 August daily at 10:00 a.m., 11:00 a.m., 2:00 p.m., 3:00 p.m.

All the year round from the main office of BUDAPEST TOURIST, 5 Roosevelt tér, Budapest, on Wednesdays and Fridays at 10:00 a.m.

City tour by open motorcoach

The 3-hour sightseeing tours start from Erzsébet tér and include Heroes Square, the Basilica, the Parliament and the Castle District. The Programme ends with a soft drink in the Citadel.

Information: OMNIBUSZ Travel Agency, Erzsébet tér.

5 June — 29 September daily at 11:00 a.m. and 2:30 p.m.

Goulash-party

A 3-hour evening programme. Apricot brandy, Hungarian Goulash soup, strudel, tasty wines. Quiz shows, Gipsy music during dinner.

Meeting points: at hotels between 6:30 and 7:15 p.m., at the Central Bus Station (Erzsébet tér, Budapest V.) between 7:15 and 7:30 p.m.

1 May—31 October.

Budapest by night from aboard a ship

An overall view of the cityscape between Petőfi Bridge and Árpád Bridge. Tourists are served coffee and champagne on board.

1 May — 30 September, on Wednesdays, Fridays and Saturdays at 9:00 p.m.

Meeting point: Vigadó tér.

Budapest by night

Sightseeing tour (in the summer season) and a night out with dinner, cocktail at a club and visiting one of Budapest's many night clubs.

All the year round on Wednesdays and Saturdays at 7:30 p.m., 1 May — 31 October daily at 7:30 p.m.

Meeting point: Central Bus Station, Erzsébet tér

Budapest city tour by boat

An overall view of the public buildings on the Danube bank between the University of Economics and Árpád Bridge. A short walk on Margaret Island. Refreshments.

Boats start from Vigadó tér, 1 May—31 October on Mondays, Wednesdays, Fridays and Sundays at 10:00 a.m.

EXCURSIONS FROM BUDAPEST INTO THE COUNTRY

Kalocsa-Solt

A whole-day programme with equestrian show. Visiting Kalocsa, the town famous for its paprika and folk art. Refreshing drinks on arrival, an organ concert, and the programme of the local folk ensemble. After lunch, an equestrian show at Solt. Tourists may also drive carriages. Wine-tasting in one of the wine-cellars.

Meeting point: at the Central Bus Station (Erzsébet tér, Budapest V.), stops Nos. 13, 14, and 15.

1 May—31 October, at 8:00 a.m.

The Danube Bend by Bus

A one-day programme to the picturesque Danube Bend: visiting the Outdor Ethnographical Museum, the Kovács Margit collection, and the Old Town at Szentendre; the citadel and Solomon's Tower in Visegrád; sightseeing in Esztergom.

Meeting point and tickets: at the main office of BUDAPEST TOURIST (5 Roosevelt tér, Budapest V.).

15 May–30 September on Thursdays at 10:00 a.m.

Tök

The tour takes 7 hours, and includes Zsámbék (ruins of the church and lamp museum), Tök (wine tasting), equestrian show, riding, and sleighing in winter.

1 December – 28 February on Sundays at 9:00

Meeting point: Central Bus Station, Erzsébet tér

Fin-de-siècle atmosphere at Szentendre

Visiting the outdoor village museum, lunch at a quaint old restaurant, museums. Driving a coach, tasting pastries at the Nosztalgia pastry-shop.

1 May – 31 October, on Saturdays at 9:00 a.m.

Meeting point: Central Bus Station, Erzsébet tér

Folklore programme aboard a Danube ship

A 3-hour sightseeing trip and dinner on board. Folk dancers and singers.

Meeting point: Vigadó tér quay

15 June–30 September, on Tuesdays, Wednesdays, Thursdays, Fridays and Saturdays at 7:30 p.m.

Excursion into the Buda Hills

The tour takes 4 hours, and offers a sight of the busy city and the Danube from the Buda Hills. The tour also includes a travel on the teleferic and a visit to the Szemlőhegy cave.

1 May – 31 October, on Thursdays at 10:00 a.m.

Buses start from Erzsébet tér Central Bus Station.

Excursion to the Danube Bend

The tour takes a whole day and starts at Szentendre with sightseeing and visiting museums. After lunch tourists get acquainted with Esztergom, the ancient royal seat. The tour also includes Visegrád and ends with wine-tasting.

1 May – 31 October, on Tuesdays, Thursdays and Saturdays at 9:00 a.m.

1 November – 30 April, on Saturdays at 9:00 a.m.

Meeting point: Central Bus Station, Erzsébet tér.

The Danube Bend by Boat

A one-day programme. By boat to Szentendre, sightseeing, a visit to the Kovács Margit collection, wine-tasting. Lunch on board. View of the Danube Bend from the Citadel at Visegrád. On the way home, cocktails and snacks on board.

Meeting point: Vigadó tér quai.

1 May–31 October, on Wednesdays and Saturdays at 8:30 a.m.

Grape harvest at Badacsony

Lunch with Gipsy music at Badacsony, a boat trip with champagne-tasting on Lake Balaton. Grape harvest on the hillslopes, must and wine-tasting. A festive dinner, folk dancers and lottery.

Meeting point: stops Nos. 13, 14, and 15 at the Central Bus Station, Erzsébet tér, Budapest, V.

1 September–31 October, on Saturdays at 9:00 a.m.

Lake Balaton

A one-day programme. Travel by bus to Tihany, sightseeing. Lunch at Badacsony. Bathing possibilities. Visiting Balatonfüred, wine-tasting.

Meeting point: stops Nos. 13, 14, and 15, Central Bus Station, Erzsébet tér, Budapest V.

1 May–31 October, on Mondays and Thursdays, at 8:00 a.m.

HUNGARY FOR HEALTH

Hungary is uniquely rich in thermal waters. Bathing and taking the waters was very popular as far back as the Roman age and later, in the Turkish period too.

Thermal waters in Hungary are especially recommended for treating locomotor diseases, gynaecological, digestive, and circulatory disorders. Places best known for their thermal springs are: Budapest, Debrecen, Hajdúszoboszló, Harkány, Hévíz, Szeged, Eger, Gyula, Hódmezővásárhely, Miskolc, Szolnok, Balf, Bükfürdő, Dombóvár, Győr, Igal, Kisvárda, Mezőkövesd, Mosonmagyaróvár, Nyíregyháza, Parádfürdő, Sárvár, and Zalakaros.

In the following we give a brief account of the largest and best equipped medicinal baths and thermal hotels, where specialists await tourists and the sick from all over the world, all the year round.

The central travel bureau for thermal hotels, called *Danubius Szálloda és Gyógyüdülő Vállalat,* is located in Budapest, at 8 Martinelli tér, 1052.

Phone: 117-0210, telex: 22-6342.

WHAT HEALTH RESORTS ARE RECOMMENDED FOR WHAT DISEASES

	Gyula	Parád	Hajdúszoboszló	Harkány	Zalakaros	Balatonfüred	Balf	Bükfürdő	Sárvár	Hévíz	Széchenyi Medicinal Baths	Király Medicinal Baths	Császár Medicinal Baths	Lukács Medicinal Baths	Rác Medicinal Baths	Rudas Medicinal Baths	ORFI	Gellért Medicinal Baths	Thermal Hotel
DISEASES OF LOCOMOTOR ORGANS	•	•	•	•	•	•	•	•	•	•		•		•		•	•	•	•
NERVOUS DISEASES																			
Neuralgia	•	•	•	•	•					•	•			•				•	
Neuritis		•	•							•	•							•	
Migraine	•	•	•							•	•							•	
Fatigue, stress	•	•	•							•	•							•	
DENTAL DISEASES	•							•		•	•		•		•				
HEART DISEASES	•	•								•					•				
GYNAECOLOGICAL DISEASES																			
Menstrual disorders										•	•							•	
Chronic adnexitis									•			•				•	•	•	
Infertility										•						•	•		
DISEASES OF THE DIGESTIVE ORGANS																			
Stomach/duodenal ulcers	•		•							•				•		•	•	•	•
Chronic cholecystitis	•		•		•				•					•					
Rehab. after stomach/intestine operation	•		•						•					•		•		•	
Psychosomatic diseases	•		•	•	•									•		•		•	
Chronic colitits	•		•	•	•				•					•		•	•	•	•
Chronic pancreatitis			•																
METABOLIC DISEASES																			
Diabetes	•		•																
Obesity	•		•																
OTHER ILLNESSES																			
Kidney stones	•		•															•	
Chronic tracheitis	•	•	•	•		•				•	•							•	
Chronic bronchitis	•	•	•	•		•				•	•	•						•	
Chronic laryngitis	•	•	•	•	•	•				•	•							•	
SPECIAL CURES																			
"Manager fitness"	•									•	•								
Cosmetology — beauty care	•									•	•								

106

Medicinal baths in Budapest

Thermal Hotel, Margaret Island (Margitsziget), Budapest 1138
Gellért Hotel, 4 Kelen-hegyi út, 1118
ORFI (National Institute for Rheumatology and Physiotherapy), 17-19 Frankel Leó út, Budapest 1027
Rudas Baths, 9 Döbrentei tér, Budapest 1013
Rác Baths, 8-10 Hadnagy utca, Budapest 1013
Lukács Baths, 25-29 Frankel Leó út, Budapest 1023
Császár Baths, 8 Árpád fejedelem útja, Budapest 1023
Király Baths, 83 Fő utca, Budapest, 1027
Széchenyi Baths, 11 Állatkerti út, Budapest 1146.

Swimming pools in Budapest

Komjádi Béla Sports Swimming Pool, 2-4 Komjádi Béla utca, Budapest 1023
Hajós Alfréd Sports Swimming Pool, Margaret Island
Palatinus (outdoor pool), Margaret Island
Római fürdő (outdoor pool)
Csillaghegy (outdoor pool), 3 Pusztakuti út, Budapest 1038
Pünkösdfürdő (outdoor pool), 272 Királylaki út, Budapest 1039
Szabadság (outdoor pool), 36 Népfürdő utca, Budapest 1138.

SPORTS, HOBBIES

Tennis Courts (in hotels)

Budapest: Flamenco (all the year round, covered court)
Budapest: Novotel
Budapest: Olympia

Horse Riding

Tourist offices and travel agencies both organize riding tours. Hungary has some of the best cross-country riding tracks in Central-Europe. For riding tours contact: IBUSZ (Budapest V, 5 Ferenciek tere); SIOTOUR (8622 Szántódpuszta. Phone: 84/31-014), and Pegazus Tours (Budapest V, 5 Ferenciek tere . Phone: 117-1552, 118-0542). Gallopping races are open from spring till autumn on Thursday and Sunday afternoons, at Budapest X, 2 Albertirsai út. Trotting races are open all the year round on Wednesdays at 4:30 p.m., and Saturdays at 2:00 p.m. at Budapest VIII, 9 Kerepesi út, near the Eastern Railway Station.

Hunting

The forests of Hungary abound in game. Information on hunting may be obtained from:
HUNTOURS — 1024 Budapest, 34 Retek utca.
Phone: 135-2313

MAVAD
1014 Budapest, 39 Úri utca. Phone: 175-9611, telex: 22-5965
VADEX (Foreign Trade Office of the Mezőföld State Forestry)
1013 Budapest, 41—43 Krisztina körút (in Hotel Buda-Penta).
Phone: 166-7652, 161-0060, Telex: 22-7653
PEGAZUS TOURS — VADCOOP
1052 Budapest, 4 Apáczai Csere János utca (in Hotel Duna Inter-Continental). Phone: 117-5122, Telex: 22-5277

Angling

Hungary is rich in waters suitable for angling. Tourists must show their passports for fishing permits. Information: MOHOSZ — (Hungarian National Angling Association), 1051 Budapest, 20 Október 6. utca. Phone: 132-5315, from Monday to Thursday 8:00 a.m. to 5:00 p.m., Friday 8:00 a.m. to 4:00 p.m. Occasional angling tickets are sold in travel agencies, tourist offices, hotels, campsites and at the local offices of the Association.

Hiking

Information on guided tours and walks:
Magyar Természetbarát Szövetség.
Information: Phone: 153-1930
Budapest VI, 31 Bajcsy-Zsilinszky út II/3.
Postal address: 1374 Budapest 5. P.O.Box 641.
Phone: 111-2467, 111-9289
Budapesti Természetbarát Szövetség
1364 Budapest V, 62—64 Váci utca. P.O.Box 29.
Phone: 118-3933 ext. 58.

Rowing, Canoeing

The most suitable waters for water tourism are the Rivers Danube and Tisza, Rába and the Körös rivers, as well as Lakes Balaton and Velence. Further information: Magyar Természetbarát Szövetség, Information Office, Budapest VI, 31 Bajcsy-Zsilinszky út.
Phone: 111-2467, or at the county offices.

Water Sports

At Balatonfüred, in the XXVII. FICC RALLY camping there is a 800-metre long *electric water-ski track,* suitable for 12 persons simultaneously. The speed can be varied between 30 and 60 km.p.h. The use of life-jackets is compulsory! Open 1 May — 31 August, every day 8:00 a.m. to 6:00 p.m.
Sailing course at the Balatonalmádi pier. Apply at:
BUDAPEST TOURIST, 1052 Budapest, 5 Roosevelt tér. Phone: 117-3555, 118-6167, telex: 22-5726.
Sellő Yacht Club
8360 Balatonboglár pier

Hiring of sailboats: at the Balatonboglár and Balatonalmádi pier, or BALATONTOURIST Veszprém, 21 Kossuth Lajos utca. Phone: 80-26-277, telex: 32-350.
MAHART Balatoni Hajózási Leányvállalat, 8600 Siófok, 2 Krúdy sétány. Phone: 84-10-050, telex: 22-5805
Hiring of *surf-boards* and *waterbikes:* in the major campsites and beaches at Lakes Balaton and Velence, and in the campsites of Express Travel Bureau: Balatonszemes, Kiliántelep, and Velence. *Surfing* courses are organized by Express Travel Bureau, Budapest V, 4 Semmelweis utca.
Phone: 117-8600, telex: 22-7108.

Stamp-Collecting

Stamp-collecting is a very popular hobby in Hungary. Purchase and sale: Magyar Filatéliai Vállalat, which has two shops in Budapest VI, 3 Oktogon, and V, 17 –19 Petőfi Sándor utca. There are shops also in major country towns and county seats. Stamps may be taken out of the country with the special permission of the customs office only. Information at any customs office. Hungarian collectors may send stamps abroad up to the value of 6,000 Forints a year. Exchange and customs formalities: Magyar Bélyeggyűjtők Országos Szövetsége, Budapest VI, 65 Vörösmarty utca.

Buying Art Objects

The Bizományi Áruház Vállalat is at your disposal: Budapest IX, 12 Kinizsi utca, headquarters. Phone: 117-6511. There is a huge network of shops selling art objects, paintings, carpets, furniture. The above enterprise also provides information on customs regulations and the export of art.

Numismatics

Hungary has a rich tradition of medal and coin collecting. The Magyar Éremgyűjtők Egyesülete (Numismatic Association of Hungary) organizes several auctions a year. Their address: Budapest VI, 77 Andrássy út. Phone: 122-3667. Export or exchange of old coins, medals, badges and decorations can be arranged through the National Bank of Hungary.

GOURMETS' DELIGHTS

Attractive restaurants, wine-cellars and inns offer delicious food and drinks — a real challenge to the palate!
A characteristic spice of Hungarian cuisine is paprika, the small, aromatic red pepper. Sour cream is used with many dishes, giving them a special flavour.
The best-known and most popular Hungarian dishes are kettlegoulash (bográcsgulyás), fish-soup (halászlé), chicken fried in batter, meat roasted on a skewer, and all kinds of wild game. Roast pike-perch (fogas) is always a real Hungarian treat.

Among the delicious Hungarian dessert offerings are apple, sweet cheese, cherry and cabbage strudel. Filled crêpes are also popular. Dobos cake — named after its "inventor", a Hungarian confectioner — is known throughout the world.
Tasty Hungarian wines top off the meal. Of these the most renowned is Tokay Aszú, the "wine of kings and the king of wines" ever since the Middle Ages. Other wines that should be tasted are the white Badacsonyi Kéknyelű, Rizling and Szürkebarát, and Egri Bikavér, a heavy red wine.

INTERNATIONAL CUISINE

ASTORIA***
(V, 19—21 Kossuth Lajos utca. Phone: 117-3411)
ATRIUM HYATT*****
(V, 2 Roosevelt tér. Phone: 138-3000)
Old Timer
Tokaj
BÉKE RADISSON****
(VI, 43 Teréz krt. Phone: 132-3300)
Szondi
BUDA-PENTA****
(I, 41—43 Krisztina krt. Phone: 156-6333)
Budavár
DUNA INTER-CONTINENTAL*****
(V, 4 Apáczai Csere János utca. Phone: 117-5122)
Bellevue Supper Club
FLAMENCO****
(XI, 7 Tas vezér utca. Phone: 161-2250)
La Bodega
FORTUNA
(I, 4 Hess András tér. Phone: 175-6857)
FORUM*****
(V, 12—14 Apáczai Csere János utca. Phone: 117-8088)
Forum Grill
GELLÉRT****
(XI, 1 Szt. Gellért tér. Phone: 185-2200)
Duna
GRAND HOTEL HUNGARIA
(VII, 90 Rákóczi út. Phone: 122-9050)
GRAND HOTEL ROYAL****
(VII, 47—49 Erzsébet krt. Phone: 153-3133)
Hársfa Room
GUNDEL
(XIV, 2 Állatkerti út Phone: 122-1002)
BUDAPEST HILTON*****
(I, 1—3 Hess András tér. Phone: 175-1000)
Kalocsa
Dominican

NOVOTEL BUDAPEST****
(XII, 63—67 Alkotás utca. Phone: 186-9588)
Karolina
TAVERNA****
(V, 20 Váci utca, Phone: 138-3522)
THERMAL HOTEL*****
(XIII, Margaret Island. Phone: 132-1100)
Platán

HUNGARIAN CUISINE

ALABÁRDOS
(I, 2 Országház utca. Phone: 156-0851)
APOSTOLOK
(V, 4—6 Kígyó utca. Phone: 118-3704)
ARANYBÁRÁNY CSÁRDA
(V, 4 Harmincad utca. Phone: 117-2703)
CSÁRDA — Hotel Duna-Intercontinental
(V, 4 Apáczai Csere János utca. Phone: 117-5122)
DUNAKORZÓ
(V, 3 Vigadó tér. Phone: 118-6362)
EMKE KALOCSA CSÁRDA
(VII, 2 Erzsébet krt. Phone: 112-9814)
FESZTIVÁL
(VI, 11 Andrássy út. Phone: 122-6075)
HÁRSFA
(II, 132 Hűvösvölgyi út. Phone: 135-0997)
KÁRPÁTIA
(V, 4—8 Ferenciek tere. Phone: 117-3596)
KISKAKUKK
(XIII, 12 Pozsonyi út. Phone: 132-1732)
MARGITKERT
(II, 15 Margit utca. Phone: 135-4791, 115-8682)
MÁTYÁS PINCE
(V, 7 Március 15. tér. Phone: 118-1650, 118-1693)
MÉNES CSÁRDA
(V, 15 Apáczai Csere János utca. Phone: 117-0803)
NEW YORK HUNGARIA
(VII, 9—11 Erzsébet krt. Phone: 122-3849)
PEST-BUDA
(I, 3 Fortuna utca. Phone: 156-9849)
PILVAX
(V, 1—3 Pilvax köz. Phone: 117-6396, 117-5902)
POSTAKOCSI
(III, 2 Fő tér. Phone: 168-7801)
RÉGI ORSZÁGHÁZ
(I, 17 Országház utca. Phone: 175-0650)
RÉZKAKAS
(V, 3 Veres Pálné utca. Phone: 118-0348, 118-0038)

SZÁZÉVES
(V, 2 Piarista utca. Phone: 118-3608)
SZEGED
(XI, 1 Bartók Béla út. Phone: 166-6503)
TABÁNI KAKAS
(I, 27 Attila út. Phone: 135-2139)
THÖKÖLY
(XIV, 80 Thököly út. Phone: 122-5444)
VÖRÖS POSTAKOCSI
(IX, 15 Ráday utca. Phone: 117-6756)

INNS

BALÁZS VENDÉGLŐ
(II. 207 Hűvösvölgyi út. Phone: 176-5516)
CIMBORÁS
(II, 4 Zöldmáli lejtő. Phone: 168-8566)
CSARNOK VENDÉGLŐ
(V, 11 Hold utca. Phone: 112-2016)
DÖMSÖDI PINCECSÁRDA
(VIII, 1/c Luther utca. Phone: 133-4535)
GARVICS VENDÉGLŐ
(II, 2 Ürömi köz. Phone: 168-3254)
NÁNCSI NÉNI VENDÉGLŐJE
(II, 80 Ördögárok utca. Phone: 116-7830)
PETNEHÁZI LOVASCSÁRDA
(II, Ady-liget, Feketefej utca. Phone: 116-4267)
PIKKELY HALÁSZCSÁRDA
(I, 29 Iskola utca. Phone: 135-6828)
RÉGI SIPOS HALÁSZKERT
(III, 46 Lajos utca. Phone: 168-6480)

WINE-CELLARS, BEER-HOUSES

ÁDÁM SÖRÖZŐ
(VI, 41 Andrássy út. Phone: 142-0358, 122-4620)
ARANYHÍD SÖRBÁR
(XI, 64 Hegyalja út. Phone: 125-1235)
ARANYHORDÓ SÖRÖZŐ-BOROZÓ
(I, 16 Tárnok utca. Phone: 136-1399)
ASTORIA GÖSSER SÖRÖZŐ
(V, 19—21 Kossuth Lajos utca. Phone: 117-3411)
BÁSTYA ÉTTEREM — Tuborg Söröző
(VIII, 29 Rákóczi út. Phone: 113-0477)
BÉCSI SÖRÖZŐ
(V, 8 Eötvös Loránd utca. Phone: 117-4504)
BORKATAKOMBA
(XXII, 64 Nagytétényi út. Phone: 226-4859)

BOWLING SÖRÖZŐ — *Hotel Novotel Budapest*
(XII, 63 Alkotás utca. Phone: 166-8007)
CITADELLA
(XI, Gellért Hill. Phone: 166-4142)
DAB SÖRÖZÖ — *Hotel Taverna*
(V, 20 Váci utca. Phone: 138-3522)
ERZSÉBET SÖRÖZŐ
(VII, 48 Erzsébet krt. Phone: 122-2040)
FREGATT SÖRÖZŐ
(V, 26 Molnár utca. Phone: 118-9997)
GÖSSER SÖRÖZŐ
(V, 1 Szende Pál utca. Phone: 118-6316)
GÖSSER SÖRPATIKA
(V, 1 Régiposta utca. Phone: 118-2608)
KALTENBERG BAJOR KIRÁLYI SÖRÖZŐ
(IX, 30—36 Kinizsi utca. Phone: 118-9792)
KASSAI SÖRÖZŐ-BOROZÓ
(XIII, 14 Pannónia utca. Phone: 112-4059, 112-8061)
KRISZTINA SÖRÖZŐ
(XII, 25 Krisztina körút. Phone: 136-3024)
KRONENBOURG BOWLING BAR
(V, 20 Váci utca. Phone: 138-3522)
MÁRVÁNYMENYASSZONY
(I, 6 Márvány utca. Phone: 175-3165)
MEGYERI CSÁRDA
(IV, 102 Váci út. Phone: 169-3964)
PEPITA OROSZLÁN
(V, 40 Váci utca. Phone: 117-4261)
PILSNER SÖRÖZŐ
(V, 25 Irányi utca. Phone: 118-2706)
RADEBERGER SÖRÖZŐ
(III, 16 Hídfő utca. Phone: 188-7399)
RONDELLA BOROZÓ
(V, 4 Régiposta utca. Phone: 118-3503)
SIPOS
(III, 2 Fő tér. Phone: 188-8745)
VASMACSKA — *Holsten söröző*
(III, 5 Laktanya utca. Phone: 188-7123)
VIGADÓ SÖRÖZŐ
(V, 2 Vigadó tér. Phone: 118-1598)
VINCELLÉR BOROZÓ — *Grand Hotel Hungária*
(VII, 90 Rákóczi út. Phone: 122-9050)

RESTAURANTS OFFERING FOOD OF FOREIGN COUNTRIES

AMERICAN CUISINE

PRÉRI STEAK HOUSE
(II, 8 Zsigmond tér. Phone: 168-8256)

ARABIAN CUISINE

ALADDIN
(VIII, 23/a Bérkocsis utca)

CHINESE CUISINE

VÖRÖS SÁRKÁNY
(VI, 80 Andrássy út. Phone: 131-8757)

CUBAN CUISINE

HABANA
(VI, 21 Bajcsy-Zsilinszky út. Phone: 112-1039)

CZECH CUISINE

PRÁGAI SVEJK VENDÉGLŐ
(VII, 59/b Király utca. Phone: 122-3278)
PRÁGAI VENCEL SÖRHÁZ
(VIII, 57/a Rákóczi út. Phone: 133-1342)

FRENCH CUISINE

ETOILE
(XIII, 4 Pozsonyi út. Phone: 112-2242)
LE JARDIN DE PARIS
(I, 20 Fő utca. Phone: 115-4431)

GERMAN CUISINE

BERLIN ÉTTEREM — RAABE-DIELE SÖRÖZŐ
(V, 13 Szent István krt. Phone: 131-0314)

ITALIAN CUISINE

NAPOLETANA
(V, 3 Petőfi tér. Phone: 118-5714)
PICCOLINO PIZZERIA — *Novotel Budapest*****
(XII, 63—67 Alkotás utca. Phone: 186-9588)

JAPANESE CUISINE

JAPÁN
(VIII, 4—6 Luther utca. Phone: 114-3427)

GREEK CUISINE

SIRTOS
(VII, 24 Csengery utca. Phone: 141-0772)

KOREAN CUISINE

SEOUL HOUSE
(I, 8 Fő utca. Phone: 201-9607)

KOSHER FOOD

HANNA
(VII, 35 Dob utca. Phone: 142-7359)
SHALOM
(VII, 2 Klauzál tér. Phone: 122-1464)

MEXICAN CUISINE

LA PAMPA
(XIII, 5—7 Pannónia utca. Phone: 131-1599)

SERBIAN CUISINE

BELGRÁD SÖRÖZŐ
(V, 13 Belgrád rakpart. Phone: 118-1815)
KISLUGAS
(II, 77 Szilágyi Erzsébet fasor. Phone: 156-4765)
SZERB VENDÉGLŐ
(V, 16 Nagy Ignác utca. Phone: 111-1858)

SLOVAKIAN CUISINE

ARANYFÁCÁN
(XII, 33 Szilágyi Erzsébet fasor. Phone: 115-1001)
SZLOVÁK SÖRÖZŐ
(V, 17 Bihari János utca. Phone: 112-3245)

PASTRY SHOPS

ANGELIKA
(I, 7 Batthyány tér. Phone: 201-4847))
ANNA
(V, Váci utca. Phone: 118-2016)
BÉCSI KÁVÉZÓ — Hotel Forum
(V, 12—14 Apáczai Csere János utca.
Phone: 117-8088)
BONBON ESZPRESSZÓ
(V, 29 Szent István krt. Phone: 132-3708)
CAFE PIERROT
(I, 14 Fortuna utca. Phone: 175-6971)

STEFÁNIA — GRAND HOTEL HUNGÁRIA
(VII, 90 Rákóczi út. Phone: 122-9050)
GERBEAUD
(V, 7 Vörösmarty tér. Phone: 118-1311)
GOURMAND
(V, 2 Semmelweis utca. Phone: 118-6516)
HAUER
(VIII, 49 Rákóczi út. Phone: 114-2032)
NEW YORK HUNGÁRIA KÁVÉHÁZ
(VII, 9—11 Erzsébet krt. Phone: 122-3849)
KORONA
(I, 16 Dísz tér. Phone: 175-6139)
LUKÁCS
(VI, 70 Andrássy út. Phone: 132-1371)
MARGARÉTA — Hotel Budapest Hilton
(I, 1—3 Hess András tér. Phone: 175-1000)
MŰVÉSZ
(VI, 29 Andrássy út. Phone: 122-4606)
RUSZWURM
(I, 7 Szentháromság utca. Phone: 175-5284)
ZSOLNAY KÁVÉHÁZ — Hotel Béke Radisson
(VI, 43 Teréz krt. Phone: 132-3300)

ENTERTAINMENT IN BUDAPEST

Music
MAGYAR ÁLLAMI OPERAHÁZ — Hungarian State Opera
(VI, 22 Andrássy út. Phone: 153-0170)
MAGYAR ÁLLAMI OPERAHÁZ ERKEL SZÍNHÁZA — Erkel
Theatre of the Hungarian State Opera
(VIII, Köztársaság tér. Phone: 133-0540)
FŐVÁROSI OPERETT SZÍNHÁZ — Municipal Operetta Theatre
(VI, 17 Nagymező utca. Phone: 132-0535)
— performances: September — end-June
Programmes in the leaflet 'Programok', available at travel agencies and hotels.

Concert halls
— performances: September — end-June
ZENEAKADÉMIA — Music Academy
(VI, 8 Liszt Ferenc tér. Phone: 142-0179)
PESTI VIGADÓ — Redoute
(V, 2 Vigadó tér. Phone: 112-9903)
BUDAPEST KONGRESSZUSI KÖZPONT — Budapest Congress Centre
(XII, 1—3 Jagelló út. Phone: 186-9588)
LISZT FERENC KAMARATEREM — Liszt Ferenc Chamber Hall
(VI, 35 Vörösmarty utca)

MTA ZENETUDOMÁNYI INTÉZET — Institute of Music of the Hungarian Academy of Sciences
(I, 7 Táncsics Mihály utca. Phone: 175-9011)
BARTÓK EMLÉKHÁZ — Bartók Memorial House
(II, 29 Csalán utca. Phone: 176-2100)
— In the summer season, concerts are held at the following places as well:
MÁTYÁS TEMPLOM — Matthias Church
(I, Szentháromság tér) — on Fridays
BUDAPESTI TÖRTÉNETI MÚZEUM — Budapest History Museum (I, 2 Szent György tér) — on Sundays at 11:30 a.m, Renaissance choir music
DOMINIKÁNUS UDVAR — Dominican Courtyard — HILTON HOTEL
(I, 1—3 Hess András tér)
HILD UDVAR — Hild Courtyard
(II, 5 Árpád fejedelem útja. Phone: 131-1311, 142-3747)
MAGYAR NEMZETI GALÉRIA
Hungarian National Gallery (Buda Castle) — on Sundays at 11:00 a.m. Choir music
Tickets at Filharmónia (V, 1 Vörösmarty tér. Phone: 117-6222)

Foreign Language Literary Evenings
KORONA PÓDIUM
(I, 16 Dísz tér) — Mondays — Thursdays

Pantomime
CENTI SZÍNPAD
(VIII, 45 Üllői út, 3rd floor) — performances of the Domino Ensemble

Puppet Theatre
MAGYAR ÁLLAMI BÁBSZÍNHÁZ — Hungarian State Puppet Theatre (Childrens' and adults' performances)
(VI, 69 Andrássy út. Phone: 142-2702)
KAMARASZÍNHÁZ — Chamber theatre
(VI, 19 Jókai tér. Phone: 112-0622)

Zoo
FŐVÁROSI ÁLLAT- ÉS NÖVÉNYKERT — Municipal Zoo and Botanical Gardens
(XIV, 6—12 Állatkerti út) — open every day

Circus
FŐVÁROSI NAGYCIRKUSZ — Municipal Circus
(XIV, 7 Állatkerti út) Performances on several occasions a week.

Planetarium, Laser Theatre
(X, Népliget — performances every day)

Fun Fair
VIDÁMPARK
(XIV, 14—16 Állatkerti út) April — September 10:00 a.m. to 8:00 p.m., September — April: 10:00 a.m. to 7:00 p.m. Open every day.

Folklore programmes
Travel bureaus organize half- and full-day folklore programmes. Information: TOURINFORM, phone: 117-9800.
Stage perfomances (folk dance, folk music)
FOLKLOR CENTRUM
(XI, 47 Fehérvári út)
Dance forum
BUDAI VIGADÓ (I, 8 Corvin tér)
Dance houses: FOLKLÓR CENTRUM (XI, 47 Fehérvári út). — On Tuesdays and Thursdays: KASSÁK KLUB (XIV, 57 Uzsoki út) — Every second Thursday: PETŐFI CSARNOK (XIV, Zichy M. út), LÁGYMÁNYOSI KÖZÖSSÉGI HÁZ (XI, 17 Kőrösy utca) — On Fridays: ALMÁSSY TÉRI SZABADIDŐ KÖZPONT (VII, 6 Almássy tér.) — On Saturdays: BELVÁROSI IFJÚSÁGI HÁZ (V, 9 Molnár utca), MOM MŰVELŐDÉSI HÁZ (XII, 18 Csörsz utca), MARCZIBÁNYI TÉRI MŰVELŐDÉSI KÖZPONT (II, 5/a Marczibányi tér).

Gipsy music is played in many restaurants from about 6:00 p.m.

Disco clubs

Name	Address	Phone	Open
Blue Box	IX, 28 Kinizsi utca	118-0983	
Expo 25 Disco	in "Expo-Town"		21—03 h
Fortuna Disco	I, 4 Hess A. tér	175-2401	Wed, Fri, S, 21—03 h (June—August every day)
Halászbástya Levis 501	I, Halászbástya	156-1446	
Dancing Club	VI, Nagymező utca/ Lovag utca	132-3857	21—04 h
Margithíd	V, 1 Szt. István krt.	112-4215	21—04 h
Mediterrán	Novotel Budapest XII, 63—67 Alkotás u.	166-8007	Thursdays Fridays
Sztár lézerdisco	Atrium Hyatt Hotel V, 2 Roosevelt tér	138-3000	21—03 h

Night drink bars

Name	Address	Phone	Open
Amazonas	Hotel Volga		
	XIII, 65 Dózsa György út	140-8393	22—04 h*
Balloon	Hotel Atrium Hyatt		
	V, 2 Roosevelt tér	138-3000	12—02 h
Budapest	Hotel Budapest		
	II, 47 Szilágyi E. fasor	115-3230	22—04 h*
Casanova	I, 4 Batthyány tér	133-8320	18—04 h
Duna-bár	In front of Forum Hotel,		
	on the Danube	117-0803	20—02 h
Éden Biliárd			
Club	I, 7 Széna tér	115-3013	22—05 h
Etoile Night			
Club	XIII, 4 Pozsonyi út	112-2242	21—04 h*
Gellért	Hotel Gellért		
	XI, 1 Szt. Gellért tér	185-2200	22—04 h*
Halászbástya	Hotel Hilton		
	I, Halászbástya	156-1446	22—04 h*
Nirvána	V, 13—15 Szt. István krt.	111-8894	
Piros Elefánt	Hotel Olympia		
	XII, 40 Eötvös út	156-8011	22—04 h*
Regina	Hotel Palace		
	VII, 43 Rákóczi út	113-6000	21—04 h*
Rokokó	Hotel Wien		
	XI, 88 Budaörsi út	166-5954	22—04 h*

* Closed on Sundays

Night clubs

Name	Address	Phone	Open
Astoria	V, 19—21 Kossuth L. utca	117-3411	22—04 h
Ballantine's			
Club	VI, 19 Andrássy út	122-7896	17—05 h
Pigalle	VII, 65 Király utca	122-4621	22—05 h
Havanna Night	Hotel Thermal		
Club	XIII, Margaret Island	111-1000	22—03 h
Horoszkóp	Hotel Buda Penta		
	I, 41—43 Krisztina krt.	156-6333	22—04 h
Maxim Varieté	VII, 3 Akácfa utca	122-7858	19,30—2,30 h
Moulin Rouge	VI, 17 Nagymező utca	112-4492	20—03 h
Orfeum	Hotel Béke Radisson		
	VI, 43 Teréz krt.	132-3300	21—04 h
Pipacs	V, 5 Aranykéz utca	118-5505	22—05 h

CASINOS

CASINO BUDAPEST HILTON — at Hilton Hotel, open daily from 5:00 p.m. French and American Roulette, Black Jack, Baccara, fortune wheel and slot machines.
Budapest I, 1—3 Hess András tér. Phone: 175-1000
Charge for admission: 10 DM.
CASINO BUDAPEST GRESHAM — American and French Roulette, Black Jack, fortune wheel and slot machines. Open daily from 2:00 p.m.
Budapest V, 5 Roosevelt tér. Phone: 117-4445
Charge for admission: 10 DM.
CASINO BUDAPEST SCHÖNBRUNN — on a ship at the Pest head of Chain Bridge. Open from 4:00 p.m.
American Roulette, Black Jack and slot machines.
Charge for admission: 10 DM.

ACCOMMODATIONS

HOTELS IN BUDAPEST

ATRIUM HYATT *****
V, 2 Roosevelt tér. Phone: 266-1234
DUNA INTER-CONTINENTAL *****
V, 4 Apáczai Csere János utca. Phone: 117-5122
GRAND HOTEL CORVINUS KEMPINSKI *****
V, 7—8 Erzsébet tér. Phone: 266-1000
HILTON HOTEL BUDAPEST *****
I, 1—3 Hess András tér. Phone: 175-1000
THERMAL HOTEL MARGITSZIGET *****
XIII, Margitsziget. Phone: 132-1100

BÉKE RADISSON ****
VI, 43 Teréz krt. Phone: 132-3300
BUDA PENTA ****
I, 41—43 Krisztina krt. Phone: 156-6333
DUNAPART SHIP-HOTEL ****
I, Szilágyi Dezső tér, Quay. Phone: 155-9001
FLAMENCO OCCIDENTAL ****
XI, 7 Tas vezér utca. Phone: 161-2250
FÓRUM HOTEL BUDAPEST ****
V, 12—14 Apáczai Csere János utca. Phone: 117-8088
GELLÉRT ****
XI, 1 Szt. Gellért tér. Phone: 185-2200
GRAND HOTEL HUNGÁRIA ****
VII, 90 Rákóczi út. Phone: 122-9050
KORONA ****
V, 12 Kecskeméti utca. Phone: 117-4111
NEMZETI ****
VIII, 4 József krt. Phone: 133-9160
NOVOTEL BUDAPEST CENTRUM ****
XII, 63—67 Alkotás utca. Phone: 186-9588
OLYMPIA ****
XII, 40 Eötvös út. Phone: 156-8011
PANORÁMA ****
XII, 21 Rege utca. Phone: 175-0522
RAMADA GRAND HOTEL ****
XIII, Margitsziget. Phone: 131-7769
THERMAL HOTEL AQUINCUM ****
III, 94 Árpád fejedelem útja. Phone: 188-6360
THERMAL HOTEL HÉLIA ****
XIII, 62—64 Kárpát utca. Phone: 129-8650
VICTORIA ****
I, 11 Bem rakpart. Phone: 201-8644

AERO ***
IX, 1—3 Ferde utca. Phone: 127-4690

AGRO ***
XII, 54 Normafa út. Phone: 175-4011
ALBA ***
I, 3 Apor Péter utca. Phone: 175-9244
ASTORIA ***
V, 19 Kossuth Lajos utca. Phone: 117-3411
AUSTROTEL BUDAPEST HOTEL PALACE ***
VIII, 43 Rákóczi út. Phone: 113-6000
BENCZÚR ***
VI, 35 Benczúr utca. Phone: 142-7970
BUDAI HOTEL NORMAFA ***
XII, 52—54 Eötvös utca. Phone: 156-3444
BUDAPEST ***
II, 47 Szilágyi Erzsébet fasor. Phone: 202-0044
EMKE ***
VII, 1—3 Akácfa utca. Phone: 122-9230
ERZSÉBET ***
V, 11 Károlyi Mihály utca. Phone: 138-2111
EXPO ***
X, 10 Albertirsai út. Phone: 184-2130
LIGET ***
VI, 106 Dózsa György út. Phone: 111-3200
ORION ***
I, 13 Döbrentei utca. Phone: 175-5418
REGE ***
II, 2 Pálos utca. Phone: 176-7311
RUBIN ***
XI, 3 Dayka Gábor utca. Phone: 185-0192
STADION ***
XIV, 1—3 Ifjúság útja. Phone: 251-2222
TAVERNA ***
V, 20 Váci utca. Phone: 138-4999
VOLGA ***
XIII, 65 Dózsa György út. Phone: 129-0200

DÉLIBÁB **
VI, 35 Délibáb utca. Phone:142-9301
ÉBEN **
XIV, 15—17 Nagy Lajos király útja. Phone: 184-0677
ERAVIS **
XI, 152 Bartók Béla út. Phone: 166-7276
GULLIVER **
XIII, 26 Béke út. Phone: 131-9570
IFJÚSÁG **
II, 1—3 Zivatar utca. Phone: 115-4260
METROPOL **
VII, 58 Rákóczi út. Phone: 142-1171

MINOL **
III, 45 Batthyány utca. Phone: 180-0777
PARK **
VIII, 10 Baross tér. Phone: 113-1420
PLATÁNUS **
VIII, 44 Könyves Kálmán körút. Phone: 133-6057
RÓZSADOMB **
II, 17 Vérhalom utca. Phone: 115-5253
STUDIUM **
X, 129 Harmat utca. Phone: 147-4147
SZÁMALK **
XI, 68 Etele út. Phone: 166-9377
TUSCULANUM **
III, 10 Záhony utca. Phone: 188-7673
WIEN **
XI, 88—90 Budaörsi út. Phone: 166-5400
ZUGLÓ **
XIV, 202—204 Nagy Lajos király útja. Phone: 251-2455

TOURIST HOTELS, PENSIONS IN BUDAPEST

AQUINCUM PANZIÓ
III, 105 Szentendrei út. Phone: 168-6426
BARA PANZIÓ
I, 34—36 Hegyalja út. Phone: 185-3445
BUDA PANZIÓ
XII, 6 Kiss Áron utca. Phone: 176-2679
BUDAI HOTEL
XII, 45—47 Rácz Aladár utca. Phone: 186-3861
CITADELLA
XI, Citadella sétány. Phone: 166-5794
CSILLAGHEGYI STRAND HOTEL
III, 3 Pusztakúti út. Phone: 168-4012
EXPRESS
XII, 7—9 Beethoven utca. Phone: 175-3082
GYOPÁR PANZIÓ
II, 9 Gyopár utca. Phone: 176-8936
HÁRSHEGYI CAMPING
II, 5—7 Hárshegyi út. Phone: 115-1482
Open: 1 May — 15 October
JAGER-TRIO PANZIÓ
XI, 20/d Ördögorom út. Phone: 185-1880
KARAVÁN CAMPING
XII, 18/b Konkoly Thege M. út
Open: 1 April — 30 Sept.
KONTÉNER ÜDÜLŐHÁZAK
III, 67 Nánási út. Phone: 188-6865
Open: 15 April — 15 October

KORONA PANZIÓ
XI, 127 Sasadi út. Phone: 181-2788
LIDO HOTEL I
III, 67 Nánási út. Phone: 188-6865
LIDO HOTEL II
III, 67 Nánási út. Phone: 188-6865
Open: 1 April — 31 October
METRO TENISZ CAMPING
XVI, 222 Csömöri út. Phone: 163-8505
Open: 1 May — 15 October
MOLNÁR PANZIÓ
XII, 143 Fodor utca. Phone: 161-1167
PANORÁMA BUNGALOWS
XII, 21 Rege utca. Phone: 175-0522
PANORÁMA PANZIÓ
II, 7 Fullánk utca. Phone: 176-4718
REMETE PANZIÓ
III, 91 Remetehegyi út. Phone: 180-3437
RÓMAI FÜRDŐ CAMPING
III, 189 Szentendrei út. Phone: 168-6260
ROSELLA PANZIÓ
XII, 21 Gyöngyvirág út. Phone: 175-7329
RÓZSAKERT CAMPING
X, 7 Pilisi utca.
Open: 1 May — 30 September
SIESTA VILLA
II, 8/a Madár utca. Phone: 142-1404
SPORT PANZIÓ
II, 9 Szépjuhászné út
TÜNDÉRHEGYI "FEEBERG" CAMPING
XII, 8 Szilassy út.
Open: 1 January — 31 December
UNIKUM PANZIÓ
XI, 13 Bod Péter utca. Phone: 186-1280
VADVIRÁG PANZIÓ
III, 18 Nagybányai út. Phone: 176-4292
ZUGLIGETI "NICHE" CAMPING
XII, 101 Zugligeti út.
Open: 1 January — 30 September

TRAVEL BUREAUS, ACCOMMODATION SERVICE OFFICES IN BUDAPEST

AUSTROPA
TRAVEL BUREAU INTERNATIONAL

1052 Budapest, 4—6 Aranykéz utca. Phone: 117-9299,
117-9268
Telex: 22-3779, telefax: 117-9333

IBUSZ

Hotel Service (day and night)
1052, 3 Petőfi tér. Phone: 118-4842, telex: 22-4941
Keleti pályaudvar (Eastern Railway Station) 1087, 11/b Baross tér. Phone: 122-5429, telex: 22-4863
Nyugati pályaudvar (Western Railway Station) 1062, 55 Teréz krt. Phone: 112-3615, telex: 22-5166
1053, 5 Ferenciek tere. Phone: 118-1120, telex: 22-5090
Déli pályaudvar (Southern Railway Station) 1122.
Phone: 155-2133, telex: 22-6364

BUDAPEST TOURIST

1051, 5 Roosevelt tér.
Phone: 117-3555, telex: 22-5726
1087, 3 Baross tér.
Phone: 133-6587, 133-8981, telex: 22-4668

COOPTOURIST

1055, 13 Kossuth Lajos tér. Phone: 112-1017
Telex: 22-4741
1111, 4 Bartók Béla út. Phone: 166-5349, telex: 22-4734
1012, 107 Attila út. Phone: 175-2937
Telex: 22-6141
1065, 17 Bajcsy-Zsilinszky út. Phone: 111-7034
Telex: 22-4649
1062, Skála Metró Áruház, 1—3 Nyugati tér. Phone: 112-4867
Telex: 22-7561

EXPRESS

1054, 16 Szabadság tér. Phone: 131-7777
Telex: 22-5384
1052, 4 Semmelweis utca. Phone: 117-8600
Telex: 22-7108
1054, 16 Szabadság tér. Phone: 131-6393
Telex: 22-6059
1085, 66 József körút. Phone: 113-5249
Telex: 22-6854
1111, 34 Bartók Béla út. Phone: 185-3173
Telex: 22-6781
1064, 55 Andrássy út. Phone: 142-5337
Telex: 22-7129
Keleti pályaudvar (Eastern Railway Station) — departure side.
Phone: 142-1772

MÁVTOURS

Headquarters: 1051 Budapest, 19 Nádor utca.
Phone: 111-4025; 131-4563; telex: 22-7554

MÁVTOURS OFFICES

1051 Budapest, 19 Nádor utca. Phone: 111-2442
Telex: 22-7554
Budapest, Keleti pu. (Eastern Railway Station),
1087 Baross tér. Phone: 142-9720 ext. 25.

MAVAD TOURS

1014, 1—3 Hess András tér. Phone: 175-1000

OMNIBUSZ Travel Agency

1051 5 Erzsébet tér, Central Bus Station. Phone: 117-2511, 117-2369, telex: 22-5326
Árpád Bridge, Bus Station. Phone: 149-7156

OTP PENTA TOURS

1051, 12 Bajcsy-Zsilinszky út. Phone: 138-2099

PEGAZUS TOURS

1053, 5 Károlyi Mihály utca. Phone: 117-1562, 117-1644
Telex: 22-4679

PHÖNIX—HARMOTOUR KFT.

Headquarters
1053 Budapest, 14/b Károlyi Mihály utca.
Phone: 117-3972, 138-3341
Telex: 22-3843; Telefax: 138-3137
Travel bureaus
1055 Budapest, 19 Szent István körút. Phone: 131-3389
1053 Budapest, 6 Kossuth Lajos utca. Phone: 117-5692
Telex: 20-2505

PROTOKOLL SERVICE—RICHTER TRAVEL

1146 Budapest, 6 Zichy Géza utca
Phone / fax: 122-7550
Radiophone: 06-60-12-259, 06-60-12260

VOLÁNTOURIST

1062, 38 Teréz körút. Phone: 132-9391
Telex: 22-6722
1091, 21 Üllői út. Phone: 138-2555
Telex: 22-6655
1137, 10 Pozsonyi út. Phone: 112-0269
Telex: 22-5078

FURTHER FACTS

ENTRY

Passport, visas
Tourists entering Hungary need valid passports and visas with two photographs.
No visas are needed for tourists from the following countries: Austria, Belgium, Bulgaria, China, Cuba, Cyprus, Czechoslovakia, Denmark, Finland, France, Germany, Great Britain, Holland, Italy, Ireland, Luxembourg, Malta, Mongolia, Norway, Nicaragua, Poland, Romania, San Marino, Spain, Switzerland, Sweden, USSR, Yugoslavia, Argentina, Chile, Canada, Greece, Korea, Monaco, Portugal, Uruguay, Ecuador, Island.

Visas are issued:
In a foreign country:
— in person at an Embassy
— by post (24 hours)
At the frontier stations:
— by automobile
— at Ferihegy Airport
— at the international boat station (1/2 to 1 hour, depending on the traffic).

Prolongation of your visa:
48 hours before the expiration of validity, at the nearest police station.

Passport:
Travel documents (passports, visas, statistical leaflets) should be kept by the tourist and presented upon request.

In case of a lost passport:
— call the nearest police station (any time), to issue a temporary document,
— on the basis of the above, your Embassy will issue a new passport,
— an exit visa is needed from the nearest police station.

STAYING IN HUNGARY

In case of injury or offence during your stay, call the police, who will issue documents needed for legal defence.

Registration:
Tourists must register only if their stay exceeds 30 days.

CUSTOMS AND EXCHANGE OF FOREIGN CURRENCY

Entry

Duty-free goods
Goods and jewels taken into the country for personal use are duty-free.

Exchange of money
There is no compulsory exchange of money in Hungary. Foreign currency can be exchanged in banks, the National Bank of Hungary, the Országos Takarékpénztár (National Savings Bank), travel agencies, hotels and campings, at the official rate established by the National Bank of Hungary. The document of exchange should be kept until leaving the country. In your own interest please change money in the above listed places only. The most popular cards are accepted in hotels, restaurants, travel agencies with a note at the entrance. The maximum amount of Eurocheque is 12.000 Forints per cheque.

Exit

Re-exchange of Forints
Remaining Forints can be re-exchanged in all major travel agencies and banks, to the maximum of the 50% of the sum previously exchanged (which sum total, however, should not exceed 100 USD).
Be sure to have proof of original exchange!

Customs prescriptions
The following goods may be taken out of the country custom-free:
— souvenirs of a value of 3.000 Forints, (max. 1.000 Forints per piece)
— goods purchased for converible currency (with a receipt) have a higher value limit.
There is a ban on foodstuffs of a value above 100 Forints, precious metals, stamps and the following: detergents, baby care goods, hosiery, cameras, moviecameras, projectors.
Permission to export art objects may be obtained from the Hungarian National Gallery, Budapest, Buda Castle, Building 'B'. Monday—Friday 9:00 a.m. — 3:00 p.m. Phone: 175-7533.

TRAVEL

How to reach Hungary

By plane

MALÉV (Hungarian Airlines) has flights to 40 cities in 30 countries. Tickets are sold at MALÉV offices.

Offices in Budapest
Reservation and tickets for MALÉV flights, Phone: 267-4333
1051 Budapest V, 2 Roosevelt tér, Phone: 266-9033
Telex: 22-4954
1051 Budapest V, 6 Dorottya utca, Phone: 267-4333
Telex: 22-5796
1051 Budapest V, 19 Apáczai Csere János utca,
Phone: 117-2911
Office for Reservation from Abroad:
1051 Budapest V, 19 Apáczai Csere János utca,
Phone: 266-5627
Telex: 22-5793.
Information:
— on flights of the day in question: 155-7155, 157-7743, 157-7695, 157-7373, 157-7484
— on foreign and MALÉV/Air France flights: 157-2122
— MALÉV departures: 157-7831, 157-8768
— MALÉV arrivals: 157-8406
Central Ferihegy telephone number (terminals 1 and 2): 157-9123.

By rail

30 international trains insure a direct link between Budapest and the major cities of Europe.
Please note: There is no visa service at the railway border crossing points! Passangers should obtain their Hungarian visas prior to departure.
Car trains
The Saxonia Express runs a daily car transport service on the Budapest — Dresden/Dresden — Budapest line during the summer season. (Not available for minibuses and caravans.)

By boat

There is a regular hydrofoil service operating between Budapest and Vienna daily between April and October, twice a day between June and mid-September. The journey takes 4.5 hours.
Tickets, reservation, information
In Vienna:
— MAHART Head Office, A—1010 Wien I., Karlsplatz 2/8.
  Phone: 43-222/50-55-644, 50-53-844. Telex: 47/13-1001
— IBUSZ, W—1010 Wien I., Krugerstr. 4.
  Phone: 43-222/51-55-50. Telex: 47/11-1113
— Erste Donau-Dampfschiffahrts-Gesellschaft (DDSG-Reisedienst), A—1010 Wien, Handelskai 265.
  Phone: 43-222/26-65-36/55. Telex: 47/13-4789.

By bus

There are regular international bus services between Hungary and eleven countries (Austria, Czechoslovakia, Germany, Greece, Holland, Italy, Poland, Romania, Soviet Union, Turkey, Yugoslavia).

Blaguss—Volánbusz
There is a daily bus service between Budapest and Vienna all the year round.
Dep. 7 a.m. Wien-Mitte, Autobusbahnhof
Arr. 11.35 a.m. Budapest, Erzsébet tér Bus Terminal
Dep. 7 a.m. Budapest, Erzsébet tér Bus Terminal
Arr. 11.35 a.m. Wien-Mitte, Autobusbahnhof.

Tickets, information
IBUSZ Reisen
Offizielles Reisebüro der Ungarischen Staatsbahnen GmbH.
A—1010 Wien I., Kärntnerstr. 26. Phone: 43-1/51-5550.
Telex: 47/11-2373.

Reisebüro Blaguss Reisen
A—1040 Wien, Wiedner Hauptstr. 15. Phone: 43-222/65-16-81.
Telex: 47/13-3869.

Deutsche Touring GmbH
D—8000 München 2, Arnulfstr. 3. Phone: 49-89/501-824/25.
Telex: 41/05-24990.

Ungarn und Osteuropareisen
D—8000 München 2, Altheiner-Eck 1. Phone: 49-89/265-020.
Telex: 41/05-24585.

IBUSZ
7000 Stuttgart, Kronprinzstrasse 6. Phone: 49/711-296233
Telex: 72-3802

By car

The IBUSZ offices at the highway border crossing stations offer visa service, currency exchange and sales of diesel coupons night and day.
Third-party insurance is compulsory in Hungary. Registration numbers and international registration letters are accepted in the case of most countries. Green cards are required from motorists of the following countries: France, Greece, Italy, Romania and Turkey. Soviet cars need a blue card.

Travel within Hungary

By plane

A tentative domestic flight service has been started between Budapest, Budaörs airport and some major towns: Kaposvár, Pécs, Debrecen, Nyíregyháza, Békéscsaba, Siófok—Balatonkiliti, Győr, Szeged. Information: 138-4867.

By rail

A considerable part of domestic transport is handled by the railways.

23 express train services operate between the capital and country towns.

Concession available for foreigners:
— group concession (min. 6 persons)
— Balaton season ticket (for 7—10 days)
— tourist season ticket (for 7—10 days)
— senior citizens' ticket for women over 55 and men over 60.

Information on rail travel

In Budapest:
— MÁV Central Information Office, 6 a.m. to 8 p.m.
Domestic travel, Phone: 122-7860, 142-9150
Foreign travel, Phone: 122-8035
— MÁV Passenger Service: Budapest VI., 35 Andrássy út. Phone: 122-8049, 122-8056.
— MÁVTOURS, Budapest VI., 35 Andrássy út. Phone: 122-8049, 122-8056.
Information services of the major railway stations:
Keleti (Eastern) Railway Station, Phone: 113-6835
Nyugati (Western) Railway Station, Phone: 149-0115
Déli (Southern) Railway Station, Phone: 175-6293

By boat

In Budapest
There are regular boat services on the Danube and on Lake Balaton from spring to late autumn, weather permitting. On the Danube, besides the MAHART excursion boats, the Budapest Transport Company also operates ferries in the city centre.

Ferries on Lake Balaton
During the summer season a ferry service operates at 40 minute intervals daily between Tihanyrév and Szántódrév from 6.20 a.m. to midnight, in off season from 6.30 a.m. to 7.30 p.m.

Information on boat services

In Budapest
MAHART Passenger Boat Service, Budapest V., Belgrád rakpart. Phone: 118-1953, telex: 22-5412.
MAHART Vigadó tér Boat Station, Phone: 118-1223
BKV Boat Station, Budapest XIII., Jászai Mari tér. Phone: 129-5844.
On Lake Balaton
MAHART Balaton Branch Office, 8600 Siófok, Boat Station. Phone: 84/12-308, telex: 22-5805.

By bus

All villages with at least 200 inhabitants can be reached by bus. There are also bus services from the bigger towns to resorts, excursion spots and spas. For departures and arrivals, contact the VOLÁN offices.

Information, ticket sales
Erzsébet Square Bus Terminal, Budapest V., Erzsébet tér. Phone: 118-2122
Domestic travel, Phone: 117-2966
Foreign services, Phone: 117-2562.

By car

TRAFFIC REGULATIONS
Traffic regulations in Hungary are generally the same as in other European countries, but the following differences should be noted:
Speed limit:

in residential areas:	60 km/h
on main roads:	80 km/h
on highways:	100 km/h
on motorways:	120 km/h

Any changes in the speed limit are indicated by signs.
— Three-point safety belts must be fitted in the front seats.
— Children under 12 may not use the front seats.
— Use of the horn is forbidden in residential areas unless there is danger of accident.
— Dimmed headlights must be used from dusk to dawn and in conditions of poor visibility in villages, urban areas and on main roads.
— In Hungary there is a total ban on alcohol in the blood while driving.
— The use of auxiliary stop lights and of dark curtains of foils in the windows is forbidden.
— Motorcyclists and pillion passengers must wear crash helmets. The use of dimmed headlight is compulsory night and day. In case of an accident the police must be called immediately. Phone: 07. Damaged vehicles may leave the country only with the permission of the police.

INSURANCE CLAIMS
Claims must be made within 48 hours of an accident, and no later than the following working day.
In Budapest:
HUNGARIA International Vehicle Insurance Office, Budapest XIV., 69 Gvadányi u., 5th fl. Phone: 252-6333.

In the country:
at country vehicle insurance branch offices.
Please note: Diesel oil can be purchased at petrol stations only for coupons. Coupons are available at IBUSZ offices, at border crossing stations and in hotels. It is advisable to calculate the required quantity of diesel oil in advance, as coupons are non-refundable.

Lead-free petrol is available at among the following petrol stations:
— Motorway M3, on the outward-bound lane, SHELL station, open night and day.
— VIII., Kerepesi út 5—7, ÁFOR station, open 6 a.m. to 8 p.m., on Sundays and holidays 7 a.m. to 3 p.m.
— Motorway M7, on the outward-bound lane, Budaörs ÁFOR station, open night and day.
— III., Mozaik utca
— V., Szabadság tér
— IX., Üllői út (ESSO)
— XI., Boldizsár utca
— XI., Tétényi út (SHELL)
— XIII., Vágány utca.
In the country:
— Balatonederics
— Balatonfüred, Széchenyi út
— Balatonvilágos, Motorway M7, at the 94 km stone
— Debrecen, István út, Motorway M4
— Gyöngyös, Szőlőskert, ÁFOR petrol station on M3 at the 75 km stone
— Győr, Tompa utca
— Hegyeshalom, Motorway M1
— Kistelek, Motorway M5
— Mátészalka
— Miskolc, Pesti út, Motorway M3
— Mosonmagyaróvár
— Pécs, Fürst Sándor utca, Motorway M6
— Sopron, Győri út
— Szentendre
— Tata, Motorway M1.

Information on road conditions:
UTINFORM
Phone: 122-7052, 122-7643. Telex: 22-6055.

Car services
There are approx. 60 car services in Budapest and in the major towns. For adresses, opening hours and a list of services contact TOURINFORM, 117-9800.

BREAKDOWN SERVICE
1. *Hungarian Automobile Club (MAK)*
In case of a breakdown call the "yellow angels" of the breakdown service.
In Budapest:
— XIV., 38/a Francia út. Phone: 252-2800 (night and day), telex: 22-4210.
There are technical stations in major country towns.
Emergency telephones along the motorways:

— on the M7 Motorway at every second km between 6 and 108 kms, 8 a.m. to 6 p.m.
— on the M1 Motorway at the 36, 63 and 83 km posts
— on the M3 Motorway at the 27, 51 and 75 km posts
In the Danube Bend:
2000 Szentendre, Belső körút, Phone: 26/11-999.
If the car cannot be repaired on the spot, the Automobile Club will tow it to the service station you indicate, or will arrange for the transport of the car abroad. Members of foreign automobile and touring clubs can pay for the expenses of the transport and repair by letter of credit.
2. *VOLÁN* (night and day)
Budapest XV., 117 Károlyi Sándor utca. Phone: 140-9326
3. *FŐSPED*
Budapest X., 3 Kőér utca. Phone: 147-5594, 157-2811 (night and day).

RENT-A-CAR SERVICE
You can rent a car for Hungary anywhere in the world from Avis, Hertz, Europcar and Budget, and in Europe, also from Inter-Rent.
Representations and agencies in Hungary
FŐTAXI—HERTZ, Budapest VII., 24 Kertész utca. Phone: 116-6116. At the airport: 157-9123.
IBUSZ—TOYOTA, Budapest V., 8 Martinelli tér. Phone: 119-4240
At the airport: 147-5754.
VOLÁNTOURIST—EUROPCAR, Budapest IX., 16 Vaskapu utca. Phone: 133-4783.
At the airport: Terminal 1, Phone: 134-2540, Terminal 2, Phone: 157-8519.
COOPTOURIST—BUDGET, Budapest IX., 43 Ferenc körút. Phone: 113-1466. At the airport: 147-7328.
Citizens of Western countries can rent cars only for foreign currency. Credit cards (Amex, Baymex, Visa, Eurocard, Eastercard) and travellers' cheques are accepted.
Conditions for car renting: The driver should be over 21, and should possess a driving licence for at least 1 year. The rental fee includes the compulsory third party insurance and maintenance fees.

City transport
In Hungary, buses handle most of the city transport, though in the capital and some big country towns (Szeged, Miskolc, Debrecen), there is also a tram and trolleybus network.

Public transport in Budapest
Tickets must be purchased in advance and validated in the machines located on all vehicles. A yellow ticket (12,—Ft) is valid for trams, trolleybuses, the Metro and HÉV (local train) services up to the city limits. A blue ticket (15,—Ft) is valid for buses.

Day passes

Day bus tickets are valid for 24 hours on buses, trams, trolley-buses, Metro and HÉV trains, within the city limits.

Day tram tickets are valid for 24 hours on trams, trolleybuses, Metro and HÉV within the city limits.

Day passes are available from tobacconists', tram and bus terminuses, at Metro ticket offices, slot-machines and at railway stations.

The *Metro* runs on 3 lines from 4.30 a.m. to 11.10 p.m.

Line No. 1: Mexikói út — Vörösmarty tér

Line No. 2: Örs vezér tere — Déli (Southern) Railway Station

Line No. 3: Kőbánya-Kispest Railway Station — Újpest.

HÉV trains serving the suburbs leave from

— Budapest, Batthyány tér—Szentendre 3.50 a.m. to 11.40 p.m.

— Budapest, Örs vezér tere—Gödöllő 4.30 a.m. to 11.35 p.m.

— Budapest, Vágóhíd—Ráckeve 3.20 a.m. to 11.34 p.m.

Other transport facilities

— Cogwheel railway, Városmajor — Széchenyi Hill 4 to 0.30 a.m., every 15 min.

— Children's railway, Hűvösvölgy — Széchenyi Hill, all the year rund

— Chairlift (Libegő), Zugliget — János Hill, 15 May to 15 September, 9 a.m. to 5 p.m., 16 Sept. to 14 May 9.30 a.m. to 4 p.m.

— Funicular (Sikló), Clark Ádám tér (Chain Bridge) — Szent György tér (Buda Castle), 7.30 a.m. to 10 p.m.

Information

For information on public transport in Budapest, traffic conditions and changed schedules ring FŐVINFORM, 117-1173 or 117-8755, night and day.

Taxi

Főtaxi: 122-2222, advance order 118-8888

Volántaxi: 166-6666

City Taxi: 153-3633

Buda Taxi: 120-0200

Rádió Taxi: 177-7777

Gábriel Taxi: 155-5000

Car parking

Two modern multi-storeyed parking facilities are at the disposal of motorists in the Inner City of Budapest, on Martinelli tér and in Aranykéz utca, open night and day.

USEFUL INFORMATION

Medical care

First aid and transport to hospitals are free for foreigners, while a charge is made for medical examination and treatment. Consulting rooms can ben found in all districts of the capital and in country towns. Foreigners are always accepted at the emergency rooms of hospitals.

Dental emergency service

Institute of Stomatology, Budapest VIII., 40 Szentkirályi u. Phone: 133-0970

Pharmacies can be found in all parts of the capital and in every village.

Some pharmacies in Budapest with night emergency service:

II., 22 Frankel Leó u.

VI., 95 Teréz krt.

VII., 86 Rákóczi út

VIII., 2 Szigony u.

IX., 121 Üllői út

IX., 3 Boráros tér

XI., 11 Kosztolányi Dezső tér

XII., 1/b Alkotás u.

XII., 4 Eötvös u.

XIV., Örs vezér tere

Ambulance: call 04 day or night.

Lost property

For information on property lost on public transport vehicles contact the BKV office at Budapest VII., 18 Akácfa u. Phone: 122-6613.

Postal services

Post offices open seven days a week (night and day):

Budapest VI., 105 Teréz körút (Western Railway Station)

Budapest VIII., 11/c Baross tér (Eastern Railway Station).

Telex:

In addition to the hotel telex services there are four public telexes in Hungary:

— Budapest V., 17/19 Petőfi Sándor utca

— Debrecen, Post Office No. 15, 18 Hajdú utca

— Keszthely, 1/3 Kossuth Lajos utca

— Miskolc, Post Office No. 4, 3/9 Széchenyi István utca

Photography

Photographic equipment and accessories are sold in OFOTÉRT shops throughout the country. Some major shops in Budapest:

— V., 14 Tanács körút

— V., 2 Váci utca

— VII., 80 Rákóczi út

Quick photo service

in the FOTEX (American-Hungarian Photo Service) shops:

— Skála Metro Department Store, V., 1—3 Nyugati tér

— Skála Budapest Department Store, XI., 6—10 Október 23 út, night and day

— VII., 2 Rákóczi út

— V., 9 Váci utca

FŐFOTO, 20 Szent István krt.
and the above OFOTÉRT shops.
Camera repairs: Budapest, VII., Akácfa utca 59.

Public holidays

New Years Day	January 1
National Day	March 15
Easter Monday	
International Labour Day	May 1
Constitution Day	August 20
National Day	October 23
Christmas	December 25—26

Foreign-language radio broadcasts

The news is broadcasted daily on the Petőfi station in English, German and Russian starting at noon.

Danubius Radio: Tourism and commercial programmes broadcast in German by Hungarian Radio from 15 April to 31 October daily from 6.30 a.m. to 10 p.m. on 100.5 MHz for Balaton and Western Hungary, and on 103.3 MHz for Budapest and Central Hungary. The programmes include travel information, music, international news and search services. Phone: 138-7840.

Esperanto News: on Sundays at 1.05 p.m. on the Bartók station. A ten-minute programme with tourist information, news, reports and current Esperanto topics.

Businessmen, Attention!

Placing your functioning capital

Joint venture regulations offer tax preference in certain areas of business. In the area of tourism, this involves three subjects:

— development of thermal and medicinal tourism in specified areas;

— renovation and utilization of protected historical mansions;

— development of hotel capacity in the capital and preferred resorts, especially in the moderate price category.

In these cases, profits of the joint venture are tax exempt for the first five years, while after the first five years of operation, the joint venture tax is only 20% instead of the usual 40%. If a previously defined part of your profits are reinvested in the venture, you will receive further tax cuts. Transfer of your hard currency home is guaranteed by the Transfer Guarantee of the National Bank of Hungary.

New regulations also make it possible for small private investors to become members of limited liability companies. Conditions: at least one Hungarian company partner, basic capital investment of at least 100,000 Forints per founding member, and a minimum of 500,000 Forints of basic starter investment.

Organization and investments of joint ventures are handled by the International Agency for Capital Investment (1014 Budapest, Babits Mihály köz 4).

Economic companies with foreign participation can get and freely use the right of ownership of the real estate needed to their activities.

Opening an account

Foreign citizens may open foreign currency accounts at several Hungarian banks such as the National Savings Bank (OTP) and others. Interest is tax exempt and all accounts are secret, and the banks will not provide any information whatsoever about them. Interest rates fluctuate according to changes in the international money market, and many from the accounts may be transferred anywhere.

The HUNGARIAN FOREIGN TRADE BANK, LTD. is one of the main commercial banks of Hungary. Clients receive the best attention in financing foreign exchange and domestic Forint transactions, in opening and handling of foreign currency accounts. The best and most competitve conditions are guaranteed.

Offices in Budapest and elsewhere:

Budapest V. Szent István tér 11
　　　　Phone:(36-1) 132-9360 or 153-4211
　　　　Telex: (61) 226941
　　　　Telefax: (36-1) 132-2568
　　　　SWIFT: MKKB HU HB

Győr　　9021 Pf. 444 or 9002 Bajcsy-Zsilinszky út 19
　　　　Phone: 06-96-18818, 06-96-15287 or 06-96-18711
　　　　Telex: 24617

Pécs　　7621 Rákóczi út 3
　　　　Phone: 06-72-32252 or 06-72-12277
　　　　Telex: 12780

Szeged　6722 Kossuth L. sugárút 8
　　　　Phone: 06-62-14377

Szolnok　5002 Pf. 32 or 5000 Kossuth Lajos utca 18
　　　　Phone: 06-56-11238 or 06-56-13215

Business hours: Monday — Friday 8 a.m. to 3 p.m.
Cashier:　　　Monday — Friday 9 a.m. to 1 p.m.

PROTOKOLL SERVICE — RICHTER TRAVEL **L**
Organization on a luxurious level of individual and group business journeys, exhibitions, courses, entertainment, hunting, both in Hungary and in Europe, by a Chevrolet bus with air condition or by airplane.
1146 Budapest, 6 Zichy Géza utca. Phone / fax: 122-7550
Radiophone: 06-60-12-259, 06-60-12-260

Where to shop
Hotel shops, Konsumtourist and Utastourist shops sell goods for foreign currencies. Credit cards are also accepted.

Works of art
Paintings, works of art, Herend china, silverware, objects of folk art and coins can be bought for convertible currency in the Konsumturist shops of the Commission Company (BÁV) in Budapest and in the country. Your receipt serves as an export permit.
Budapest I., 3 Hess András tér, phone: 175-0392
Budapest VI., 27 Andrássy út, phone: 142-5525
Szentendre, Bogdányi utca 13, phone: 26/10-690
Szombathely, Mártírok tere 10
Sopron, Színház utca 5, phone: 99/12-731
Nagykanizsa, Lenin utca 8
Wholesalers' shops:
Works of art and furniture:
KONSUMEX Foreign Trade Company
Budapest XIV., 162 Hungária körút. Phone: 122-2655, Telex: 22-5151.
Paintings:
ARTEX Foreign Trade Company
Budapest V., 31 Nádor utca
Phone: 153-0222, Telex: 22-4951.
Auctions are held in March during the Spring Festival and in July—August. For information contact:
Central BÁV (Commission) shop, IX., 12 Kinizsi utca. Phone: 117-6511
BÁV shop, V., 1—3 Bécsi utca. Phone: 117-2548.
Shops selling art and antiques for Forints:
V., 1—3 Bécsi utca, phone: 117-2548
V., 1—3 Kossuth Lajos utca, phone: 117-3718
V., 3 Szent István körút, phone: 131-4534
V., 3 Felszabadulás tér, phone: 118-3381.

Shopping in the Inner City
In addition to pleasant restaurants, pastry-shops and entertainment spots, Váci utca and Vörösmarty Square await visitors with a wide range of shops.
CLARA ROTSCHILD FASHION SHOP, HAUTE COUTURE
V., 12 Váci utca, phone: 118-4090
ADLER
V., 6 Váci utca, phone: 118-4163
BENETTON
V., 3 Párisi utca, phone: 118-5280
FONTANA
V., 16 Váci utca, phone: 118-9166
LUXUS DEPARTMENT STORE
V., 3 Vörösmarty tér, phone: 118-2277
OSTERMANN
V., 11 Váci utca, phone: 118-5160

Folk art objects
Folk Art Centre, V., 14 Váci utca
V., 13 Kecskeméti utca
V., 5 Kálvin tér
V., 14 Váci utca
V., 12 Régiposta utca
XIII., 26 Szent István körút

Foreign language books
I., 4 Hess András tér (LITEA)
V., 2 Petőfi Sándor utca (Paris Arcade)
V., 10 Váci utca
V., 32 Váci utca
V., 4 Kossuth Lajos utca
V., 18 Kossuth Lajos utca
V., 4 Vörösmarty tér

Shops specializing in maps
VI., 37 Bajcsy-Zsilinszky út
VII., 1 Nyár utca

Food and liquor stores
Special Hungarian wines and spirits are sold at several shops, including V., 11 Régiposta utca

Supermarkets open on Sundays:
ABC-food store, I., Batthyány tér	7 a.m. to 1 p.m.
ABC-food store, XIII., 30 Szent István körút	7 a.m. to 1 p.m.
Klauzál Square Skála Market, VII., Klauzál tér	8 a.m. to 2 p.m.
Supermarket of the Sugár Department Store, XIV., Örs vezér tere	7 a.m. to 1 p.m.
Erzsébet Department Store, XX., 33 Kossuth Lajos utca	8 a.m. to 1 p.m.

Kispest Department Store,
XIX., 4—5 Kossuth tér   8 a.m. to 1 p.m.
Markets
IX., 1—3 Vámház körút
Flea market, XIX., 156 Nagykőrösi út at Ecseri út, second-hand goods.
Small delicatessen shops open round the clock can be found on several spots of the city.
Most of the candy stores, florists and tobacconists are open on Sunday in the capital.
On Sunday mornings some restaurants and pastry-shops also sell milk and bread.

CALENDAR OF EVENTS

JANUARY
Budapest
Traditional New Year's concert in the ballroom of the Budapest Hilton
Nagyvázsony
Pál Kinizsi Memorial Ball

FEBRUARY
Debrecen
Hajdúság Carnival — revival of old carnival folk customs, gastronomic events
Kaposvár
"Dorottya" Ball

MARCH
Budapest
Budapest Spring Festival — 10 days, 100 venues, 1000 events (Concerts, theatre performances, folk-art shows, exhibitions, tourists' programmes)
Szentendre
Szentendre Spring Days
Sopron
Sopron Spring Days
Kecskemét
Kecskemét Spring Days
Budapest
TRAVEL — International Tourist Exhibition

APRIL
Budapest
AGROMASEXPO — International Exhibition of Agricultural and Food Industry Machinery and Instrument
HUNGAROPLAST — International Exhibition of Rubber and Synthetic Material Processing
LIMEXPO — International Light Industry Machinery Exhibition

Hollókő — Easter festivities

MAY
Budapest
Budapest International Fair, capital goods fair
Siófok — Balatonfüred
Opening of the season at Lake Balaton — national chorus festival, folk art and sports events, yachting race
Sümeg
Equestrians shows, tilt tournament
Somogybabod
Off Road Festival

JUNE—JULY
Őriszentpéter
Őrség Fair — folk art shows, traditional fair
Szombathely
International Ballroom Dancing Competition and Hungarian Championship
Miskolc
Collegium Musicum concert in the Avas Church
Visegrád
Visegrád Castle Festival — historic pageant reviving the age of King Louis the Great, equestrian shows
Sopron
Sopron Festival Weeks — chamber choir festival, organ recitals, opera performances, folk art fair, gastronomic events, Oldtimer Auto Rally, light music concerts

JUNE—SEPTEMBER
Tihany
Organ recitals in the Abbey
Szántódpuszta
St. James Day Fair, folk art fair and other events

JULY
Győr
Summer in Győr — performances on the Floating Stage, classical music concerts, folk art fair, pop concerts
Pécs
Pécs Summer Theatre — folk dance shows on the open-air stage, literary evenings in the Anna Courtyard, theatre performances at the Tettye ruins, concerts in the Cathedral
Martonvásár
Beethoven concerts in the park of the Brunszvik Mansion
Hortobágy
Hortobágy International Equestrian Days — international show jumping competition, equestrian display, four-in-hand driving, folk art shows and fair

Pécs
Industrial Fair
Nyírbátor
Nyírbátor Music Days, oratorios in the church
Eger
Agria Days — open-air performances, folklore shows
Budapest
Opera and operetta performances, folklore shows, rock operas and concerts on the open-air stages and in the Dominican Courtyard of the Hilton Hotel
Szeged
Szeged Open-air Festival
Balatonfüred
International Anna Ball
Zsámbék
Zsámbék Saturdays — theatre performances, folk art programmes, exhibitions, programmes for children, sports events
Szentendre
Summer in Szentendre
Apajpuszta
Kiskunsági Pastoral and Equestrian Days — cross-country driving competitions for two- and four-horse teams, show jumping, barbecue
Keszthely
Chamber music concerts in the Festetics Mansion and the Carmelite Church
Boglárlelle
Summer Theatre
Gyula
Gyula Castle Theatre — histories, comedies, opera performances
Kőszeg
Castle Theatre Evenings — performances in the Jurisich Castle

JULY—AUGUST
Debrecen
Debrecen Jazz Days
Esztergom
Summer in Esztergom
Organ recitals and choral concerts in the Basilica
Kőröshegy
"Cantus Pannonicus" concert series
Miskolc
Miskolc Music Summer
Nagyvázsony
Equestian Show
Veszprém
Veszprém Musical Courtyard
Mogyoród
"Formula 1" Hungarian Grand Prix

Hortobágy
Hortobágy Bridge Fair — equestrian shows, shepherds' gathering, folk art fair
Debrecen
Flower Carnival
August 20, Budapest
Constitution Day and Festival of the New Bread — open-air performances, aerial and aquatic parade in front of the Parliament building, fireworks

SEPTEMBER
Budapest
Budapest International Fair for consumer goods
Do it yourself! — International hobby and gardening show
Interplayexpo — International Toys and Teaching Aids Exhibiton on the Fair Grounds
Budapest Arts Weeks — concerts, theatre, dance and film premieres, exhibitions
Budapest Music Weeks — concerts at the Academy of Music, the Budapest Convention Centre, the Pest Concert Hall, in the Matthias Church and in the State Opera House. The opening concert is traditionally held on September 25, the anniversary of Bartók's death

SEPTEMBER—OCTOBER
Grape harvesting festivities in a number of country towns

DECEMBER
Pannonhalma
Christmas organ recital in the Abbey Church
Budapest
Midnight mass in the Matthias Church

FOREIGN REPRESENTATIONS IN HUNGARY

AUSTRALIA	1062 Budapest
	30 Délibáb utca
	Phone: 153-4233
AUSTRIA	1068 Budapest
	16 Benczúr utca
	Phone: 122-9467
BELGIUM	1015 Budapest
	34 Donáti utca
	Phone: 201-1571
BRAZIL	1118 Budapest
	3 Somlai út
	Phone: 166-6044
BULGARIA	1124 Budapest
	15—17 Levendula utca
	Phone: 156-6378

CANADA	1121 Budapest 32 Budakeszi út Phone: 167-7711	MEXICO	1021 Budapest 55/d Budakeszi út Phone: 176-7598
CHINA	1068 Budapest 17 Benczúr utca Phone: 122-4872	NICARAGUA	1021 Budapest 55/d Budakeszi út Phone: 176-7953, 176-7397
COLUMBIA	1024 Budapest 43—45 Mártírok útja Phone: 201-3448	NORWAY	1122 Budapest 35 Határőr út Phone: 155-1811
CUBA	1021 Budapest 55/d Budakeszi út Phone: 176-7953	PERU	1122 Budapest 5 Tóth Lőrinc utca Phone: 155-4019
CZECHIA	1067 Budapest 61 Rózsa utca Phone: 132-5589	POLAND	1068 Budapest 16 Városligeti fasor Phone: 122-8437
SLOVAC REPUBLIC	1143 Budapest 22 Stefánia út Phone: 163-6600	PORTUGAL	1024 Budapest 43—45 Margit körút Phone: 201-1855
DENMARK	1122 Budapest 37 Határőr út Phone: 155-7320	ROMANIA	1146 Budapest 72 Thököly út Phone: 122-7689
GERMANY	1142 Budapest 101—103 Stefánia út Phone: 251-8999	SPAIN	1067 Budapest 13 Eötvös utca Phone: 153-1011
GREAT BRITAIN	1051 Budapest 6 Harmincad utca Phone: 118-2888	SWEDEN	1146 Budapest 27/a Ajtósi Dürer sor Phone: 122-9880
FINLAND	1118 Budapest 16/a Kelenhegyi út Phone: 185-0700	SWITZERLAND	1143 Budapest 107 Stefánia út Phone: 122-9491, 122-9492
FRANCE	1062 Budapest 27 Lendvay utca Phone: 132-4980	TURKEY	1014 Budapest 45 Úri utca Phone: 155-0737
GREECE	1063 Budapest 3 Szegfű utca Phone: 122-8004	URUGUAY	1023 Budapest 12—16 Vérhalom utca Phone: 136-8333, 115-0025
HOLLAND	1146 Budapest 31 Abonyi utca Phone: 122-8432	USA	1054 Budapest 12 Szabadság tér Phone: 112-6450
INDIA	1025 Budapest 14 Búzavirág utca Phone: 115-3243	RUSSIAN FEDERATION	1062 Budapest 35 Bajza utca Phone: 132-0911, 132-4748
ITALY	1143 Budapest 95 Stefánia út Phone: 121-2450	VENEZUELA	1023 Budapest 12—16 Vérhalom utca Phone: 135-3562
ISRAEL	1026 Budapest 8 Fullánk utca Phone: 176-7896	YUGOSLAVIA	1068 Budapest 92/b Dózsa György út Phone: 142-0566, 122-9838
JAPAN	1024 Budapest 58 Rómer Flóris utca Phone: 156-4533		

TOURIST INFORMATION

Szalontai Publishing House, Budapest

Publisher: Rózsa Szalontay

Managing editor: Rózsa Szalontay ©

Text: István Lázár
The History of Budapest, and Buda Castle: József Bessenyei
Captions, Sights to See: Gabriella Szvoboda-Dománszky

Art historian consultant: Gabriella Szvoboda-Dománszky

Typography: Vera Köböl

Editorial staff: Sándor Antal, Loránd Bereczky, József Bessenyei,
István Fodor, Tamás Hoffmann, Éva Moskovszky, Györgyi Simon,
Rózsa Szalontay, Gabriella Szvoboda-Dománszky, Tamás Vízkelety

Translation: Lídia Dobos

Fotos:
Melitta Bach: 4, 66, 67
Lóránt Bérczi: 20, 21, 22, 25, 41, 64, 65, 82, 83, 107, 110, 112, 113,
114
László Budaházi: 33
János Eifert: 80
Lajos Gál: 52, 61, 71
László Gyarmathy: 121, 122, 123
László Haris: 19
Károly Hemző: 10, 23, 31, 38, 43, 45, 46, 51, 75, 100, 143
Ilona Cs. Király: 1
Antal Kiss: 7, 73, 95, 126, 133, 109
Guido Kónya: 6, 35
Lajos Köteles: 39, 40, 42, 106
Andrea Németh: 18
Alfréd Schiller: 13, 14, 15, 16, 17, 28, 29, 135, 136, 137, 138, 140,
141, 142
Miklós Sehr: 24, 30, 48, 63, 77, 99, 128, 129
József Szabó: 37, 47
Zsolt Szabóky: 8, 56, 68
Károly Szelényi: 2, 11, 57, 78, 89, 93, 96, 111, 115, 116, 117, 118,
124, 139, 148
László Szelényi: 9
János Szerencsés: 3, 5
Gyula Tahin: 36
IPV and MTI Archives

On the cover:
János Eifert: View of Budapest as seen from the tower of Matthias
Church
On the back cover:
Csaba Gábler: Jewel from the 18th century — Triton and Amphitrite

ISBN 963 8077 03 4

Offset and Playing Cards Printing Office, Budapest
Manager: Lénárd Miklós